THREE-DIMENSIONAL PIECED QUILTS

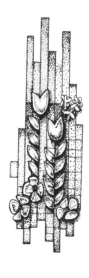

OTHER BOOKS AVAILABLE FROM CHILTON

Robbie Fanning, Series Editor

Contemporary Quilting
Appliqué the Ann Boyce Way
Barbara Johannah's Crystal Piecing
Contemporary Quilting Techniques, by
  Pat Cairns
Fast Patch, by Anita Hallock
Fourteen Easy Baby Quilts, by
  Margaret Dittman
*Machine-Quilted Jackets, Vests, and
  Coats,* by Nancy Moore
Pictorial Quilts, by Carolyn Vosburg
  Hall
*Precision Pieced Quilts Using the
  Foundation Method,* by Jane Hall
  and Dixie Haywood
*Quick-Quilted Home Decor with Your
  Bernina,* by Jackie Dodson
*Quick-Quilted Home Decor with Your
  Sewing Machine,* by Jackie Dodson
The Quilter's Guide to Rotary Cutting,
  by Donna Poster
Quilts by the Slice, by Beckie Olson
Scrap Quilts Using Fast Patch, by
  Anita Hallock
Speed-Cut Quilts, by Donna Poster
Stitch 'n' Quilt, by Kathleen Eaton
Super Simple Quilts, by Kathleen
  Eaton
*Teach Yourself Machine Piecing and
  Quilting,* by Debra Wagner
Three-Dimensional Appliqué, by Jodie
  Davis

Craft Kaleidoscope
Creating and Crafting Dolls, by Eloise
  Piper and Mary Dilligan
Fabric Painting Made Easy, by Nancy
  Ward
*How to Make Cloth Books for
  Children,* by Anne Pellowski
Jane Asher's Costume Book
Quick and Easy Ways with Ribbon, by
  Ceci Johnson
Learn Bearmaking, by Judi Maddigan
Soft Toys for Babies, by Judi
  Maddigan
Stamping Made Easy, by Nancy
  Ward
*Too Hot To Handle? Potholders and
  How to Make Them,* by Doris L.
  Hoover

Creative Machine Arts
ABCs of Serging, by Tammy Young
  and Lori Bottom
The Button Lover's Book, by Marilyn
  Green
Claire Shaeffer's Fabric Sewing Guide
*The Complete Book of Machine
  Embroidery,* by Robbie and Tony
  Fanning
Creative Nurseries Illustrated, by
  Debra Terry and Juli Plooster
Distinctive Serger Gifts and Crafts, by
  Naomi Baker and Tammy Young
The Fabric Lover's Scrapbook, by
  Margaret Dittman
*Friendship Quilts by Hand and
  Machine,* by Carolyn Vosburg Hall
Gail Brown's All-New Instant Interiors
Gifts Galore, by Jane Warnick and
  Jackie Dodson
*Hold It! How to Sew Bags, Totes,
  Duffels, Pouches, and More,* by
  Nancy Restuccia
How to Make Soft Jewelry, by Jackie
  Dodson
Innovative Serging, by Gail Brown
  and Tammy Young
Innovative Sewing, by Gail Brown
  and Tammy Young
The New Creative Serging Illustrated,
  by Pati Palmer, Gail Brown, and
  Sue Green
*Owner's Guide to Sewing Machines,
  Sergers, and Knitting Machines,* by
  Gale Grigg Hazen
Petite Pizzazz, by Barb Griffin
Putting on the Glitz, by Sandra L.
  Hatch and Ann Boyce
Quick Napkin Creations, by Gail
  Brown
Second Stitches: Recycle as You Sew,
  by Susan Parker
Serge a Simple Project, by Tammy
  Young and Naomi Baker
Sew Any Patch Pocket, by Claire
  Shaeffer
Sew Any Set-In Pocket, by Claire
  Shaeffer
Sew Sensational Gifts, by Naomi
  Baker and Tammy Young
Sew, Serge, Press, by Jan Saunders

*Sewing and Collecting Vintage
  Fashions,* by Eileen MacIntosh
Simply Serge Any Fabric, by Naomi
  Baker and Tammy Young
*Singer Instructions for Art Embroidery
  and Lace Work*
*Soft Gardens: Make Flowers with Your
  Sewing Machine,* by Yvonne Perez-
  Collins
*The Stretch & Sew Guide to Sewing
  on Knits,* by Ann Person
Twenty Easy Machine-Made Rugs, by
  Jackie Dodson

Know Your Sewing Machine, by Jackie Dodson
Know Your Bernina, second edition
Know Your Brother, with Jane
  Warnick
Know Your Elna, with Carol Ahles
Know Your New Home, with Judi
  Cull and Vicki Lyn Hastings
Know Your Pfaff, with Audrey
  Griese
Know Your Sewing Machine
Know Your Singer
Know Your Viking, with Jan
  Saunders
Know Your White, with Jan Saunders

Know Your Serger Series, by Tammy Young and Naomi Baker
Know Your baby lock
Know Your Pfaff Hobbylock
Know Your Serger
Know Your White Superlock

Star Wear
Embellishments, by Linda Fry Kenzle
Make It Your Own, by Lori Bottom
  and Ronda Chaney
Sweatshirts with Style, by Mary
  Mulari

Teach Yourself to Sew Better, by Jan Saunders
A Step-by-Step Guide to Your Bernina
*A Step-by-Step Guide to Your New
  Home*
*A Step-by-Step Guide to Your Sewing
  Machine*
A Step-by-Step Guide to Your Viking

THREE-DIMENSIONAL PIECED QUILTS

JODIE DAVIS

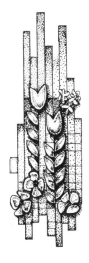

Chilton Book Company
Radnor, Pennsylvania

Designed by Anthony Jacobson
Interior art by Barbara A.C. Hennig
Color photography by Talmadge Rutlege Photography

Manufactured in the United States of America

Library of Congress Cataloging-in-Publication Data
Davis, Jodie, 1959–
     Three-dimensional pieced quilts/ Jodie Davis.
        p.   cm.—(Contemporary quilting)
     Includes bibliographical references.
     ISBN 0-8019-8390-8
     1. Patchwork—Patterns.   2. Patchwork quilts.   I. Title.
   II. Title: 3-dimensional pieced quilts.   III. Series.
   TT835.D375   1995
   746.46—dc20   94-34910
                                                   CIP

1 2 3 4 5 6 7 8 9 0   4 3 2 1 0 9 8 7 6 5

Acknowledgments

Special thanks to Kathy Semone for being my idea sounding board.

Thanks to Dorothy Buerkle for machine quilting Lone Star, Swirling
Fans, Flower Basket, Twisted Ribbons, and the Frayed Interlocking
Squares.

To Christie
You are the true meaning of "sister"

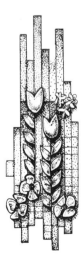

Contents

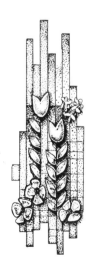

Foreword

We all know couples that, from the outside, mystify. "What does she see in him?" we whisper. "Why is he attracted to her?" I asked these questions of the sister of a woman in one such couple, wondering how the two had lasted through long separations and a seemingly unfathomable relationship.

"They're very playful together," she replied.

That explained it all to me. If anything keeps your mind loose and your spirit young, it's playfulness. And that's what I like about Jodie Davis's books. They are fun, they are whimsical, and they are playful.

This one, like *Three-Dimensional Appliqué*, plays with the notion of quilt patterns and with the use of fabric. The close-up of Twisted Ribbons on the cover of this book will give you a hint of what's inside. I found Grandmother's Flower Garden in particular a delightful surprise.

Maybe there are parallels between couples and quiltmakers. Maybe the ones who last are the most playful.

Robbie Fanning
Series Editor

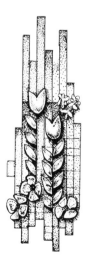

Are you interested in a quarterly newsletter about creative uses of the sewing machine and serger, edited by Robbie Fanning? Write to The Creative Machine, PO Box 2634-B, Menlo Park, CA 94026.

Introduction

What is three-dimensional piecing? My definition may surprise you.

Quilts are inherently two-dimensional, flat objects, like the cloth they are created from. Quilters have long sought to challenge this limitation by incorporating color, quilting, shape, and texture in their quilts. They have even taken this a step farther by designing block patterns that create the illusion of a third dimension. The tumbling block pattern is a familiar example. In that pattern, progressing and receding lines of perspective, as well as fabrics carefully chosen to simulate shading, transform 60° trapezoids into four-sided blocks, tumbling toward the viewer.

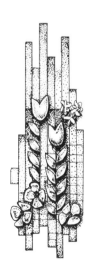

This clever use of illusion is not what you will find in this book.

The quilts I have made for *Three-Dimensional Pieced Quilts* actually incorporate a third dimension onto the surface of the quilt. Bits and pieces of cloth extend from the quilt top in various ways, literally adding texture and relief. No optical illusions here.

This is the second title in my exploration of three-dimensional quiltmaking. In experimenting with quilts for my first book, *Three-Dimensional Appliqué*, I found some of the ideas called for piecing rather than appliqué. So, this time, instead of constructing individual shapes to be appliquéd onto the quilt top, I have stuffed, gathered, folded, and tucked fabric as I pieced it to *create* the quilt top. The results have been fun and surprising. Both traditional and contemporary designs have taken on new life. A pieced pattern can become one of not just great design, color, and surface texture, but also relief!

As a bonus, these techniques make construction much easier than with the traditional methods. Thanks to the freedom and room for error these techniques afford, many of the quilts in this book are good beginner projects. The designs that incorporate gathering, for example, hide any imperfections in piecing.

As I explore various aspects of three-dimensional quiltmaking, I find that virtually every pieced and appliquéd pattern can be made using three-dimensional quilting techniques. (I say "virtually" in case I find a pattern that doesn't lend itself to my techniques. So far I haven't met such a pattern—I feel a challenge coming on.)

I've added a new feature to this book. Sprinkled throughout are pointers on how to design a quilt. If you find the process of three-dimensional piecing inspiring, you may want to go beyond the specific designs in this book and create your own. Yet, you may not be sure how to begin. In the boxes throughout the book I explain just how I puzzle out a new technique and a new design to create a finished quilt. There's no need to follow my methods exactly. Just use them to jostle your own creativity and spring into action.

I've designed twelve quilts for you and have provided complete instructions and full-size patterns for each of them. Try out my patterns or use them as inspiration to delve into your own exploration of three-dimensional piecing.

Jodie Davis

Gainesville, Virginia

The Basics

Here are the tools and skills you will need to make the projects in this book. Start with basic sewing skills, mix in a bit of a quilting background, then add a dash of enthusiasm, and you can make any project you choose. Just follow the instructions one step at a time.

General Supplies

Sewing Machine: Though not essential, a sewing machine speeds up and eases many steps in the construction process. Clean and oil your machine before each project and change to a new size 12 or 80 needle.

Bent-handle Dressmaker's Shears: A good quality pair of shears makes your cutting and trimming tasks a breeze. To keep them sharp, wipe them frequently with a soft cloth.

Rotary Cutter: If you haven't yet joined the ranks of dedicated rotary cutter fans, get one. You'll wonder how you ever got along without it.

Scissors: Use these for cutting your patterns.

Seam Ripper: A necessary evil for those inevitable mistakes—yes, even after years of sewing.

Straight Pins: Regular pins are essential. Long quilting pins will prove helpful.

Hand-sewing Needles: For general hand sewing choose size 8–10 sharp.

General Purpose Thread: Don't skimp on quality. Choose a regular sewing thread in all-cotton or cotton-covered polyester.

Thimble

Stuffing Tool: For the three-dimensional diamonds in Lone Star. My favorite is the Stuff-It (see Sources).

Marking Tools: For light fabrics I use either a 2B lead pencil or a disappearing (not wash-out) purple marker. Many quilters steer clear of the wash-out, and some even avoid the disappearing markers, because the long-term effects of the purple ink on fabric and batting are as yet unknown. For dark fabrics choose a white or silver pencil available from any quilt shop or catalog.

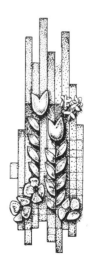

Fray-stopping Liquid: A liquid that dries clear and secures seam allowances to prevent fraying. Fray Check is a popular brand.

Batting: Over time quilters develop definite opinions on batting brands and types. My current favorites are Hobbs Polydown (100% polyester) and Heirloom Cotton (80% cotton/20% polyester). The Polydown batting quilts nicely; the machine glides across it. With a 5% shrinkage, the Heirloom Cotton batting produces the puckered look of antique quilts when the finished quilt is washed.

Dressmaker's Tracing Paper: For tracing the patterns from the book.

Template Material: Depending upon the amount of use or accuracy needed, I use either template plastic or cereal boxes for my templates. Template plastic, available in crafts and sewing stores, retains its shape, whereas the cardboard is free but wears out along the edges after repeated tracings. This distinction isn't very important for the free-form appliqués found in these projects but would cause all sorts of problems in a pieced block.

Glue Stick: To secure paper patterns to template material.

How to Transfer Patterns

The easiest way to transfer patterns is to copy them on a copy machine. Make sure the machine copies them true to size. Or you can trace the patterns from the book onto a piece of plain white paper.

Cut out your tracings and glue them to the plastic or cereal box cardboard template material. Cut the plastic or cardboard along the cut lines on the paper.

Identify the patterns by including the quilt name, pattern piece name, and any other markings on the pattern in the book. (If you copied the patterns on a copy machine, this step is already completed.)

Fabric Preparation

Prewash all cotton, cotton-blend, and other washable fabrics before cutting them out. Run them through a wash cycle, checking the rinse water for colorfastness. Remove the fabric from the dryer while still slightly damp. Iron. For fabric pieces that don't hold their shape well, use fabric spray starch.

Quilting and Binding

Because quilting and binding are beyond the scope of this book, I have included several titles in the Bibliography that treat these and other subjects in-depth and are excellent additions to any quilter's bookshelf.

Old Favorites in Three Dimensions

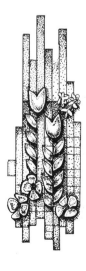

Pocket Drunkard's Path

This three-dimensional version of the Drunkard's Path quilt eases the piecing process, eliminating the need to match and stitch those tricky curved edges.

Instead, pairs of identical "path" pieces are stitched right sides together along their curved edges. Then they are turned right side out, pressed, and laid on top of the background blocks. Their raw edges are stitched into the long straight seams that join the blocks. That's it! The path then is an additional layer on top of the easily pieced background of squares.

= Background   = Path   = Border

Fig. 1-1 *Pocket Drunkard's Path*

The finished size of the Pocket Drunkard's Path quilt is 29″ (73.5 cm) square.

Materials

¾ yard (.69 m) background fabric
Thread to match background fabric
1 yard (.92 m) "path" fabric
Thread to match path fabric
1¼ yards (1.15 m) border and binding fabric
⅞ yard (.80 m) backing fabric
Batting

Instructions

Note: *All seam allowances are ¼″ (6 mm) unless specified otherwise. Pattern pieces appear at the end of the chapter.*

1. Prepare the fabrics and patterns as instructed in "Fabric Preparation" and "How to Transfer Patterns" in The Basics.

2. From the background fabric cut eighty-four 3½″ (9 mm) squares for the background blocks (see Fig. 1-1).

3. Using the patterns you've prepared, cut 48 concave and 32 convex path pieces from the path fabric.

4. With right sides facing, match the curved edges of two convex path pieces. Stitch along curved edge (Fig. 1-2). Trim seam allowances to ⅛″ (3 mm). Turn right side out. Press.

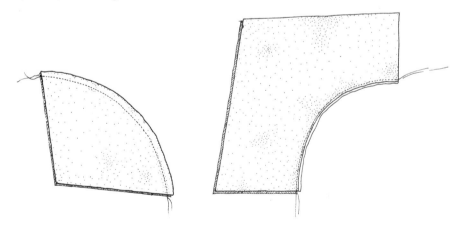

Fig. 1-2 *With right sides facing, match and stitch the curved edges of each pair of convex and each pair of concave path pieces to create two-layer pieces.*

5. Repeat Step 4 for the remaining convex pieces and all concave pieces.

6. Match the raw, straight edges of each of the two-layer concave and convex path pieces to the edges of a background block and baste as shown in Figure 1-3.

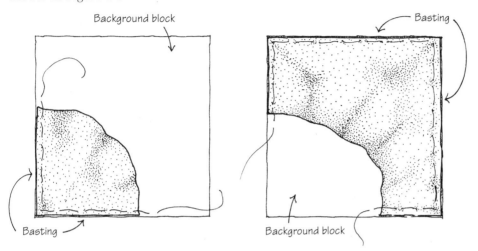

Fig. 1-3 *Lay the stitched path pieces on the background blocks. Match the straight, raw edges of the path piece to the background piece. Baste.*

7. From the border fabric cut twenty 3½" (9 cm) squares.

Yes, You Can Do It

From reactions to my quilts, I understand that many quilters have absolutely no idea of just how the design process happens. They don't know where to start or where to get ideas; many even think "I could never do that."

If you're curious, but a bit timid, please go ahead and give yourself permission to experiment. When facing something new, I ask myself, "What's the worst that could happen?" In this case, you might waste some time and fabric. That's all. But, chances are, it won't be a waste. You'll be taking your first step in a rewarding journey that will be a lot of fun and could lead to an original quilt design.

8. Starting at the top left-hand corner of the quilt and consulting the quilt diagram (Fig. 1-4a), piece each vertical row in turn (Fig. 1-4b), including border, background, and path/background pieces as indicated (Fig. 1-4c).

9. Stitch the rows together to form the quilt top (Fig. 1-5). Press.

10. Trim the outside edges of the quilt from corner to corner of the border blocks to make them into triangles (Fig. 1-6).

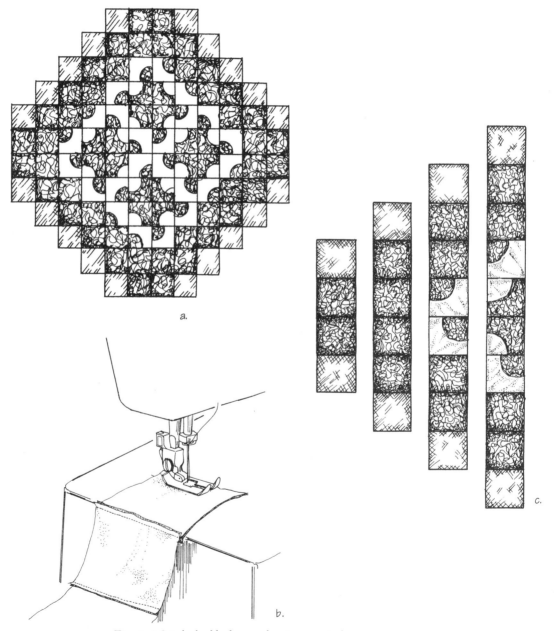

Fig. 1-4 *Stitch the blocks together into vertical rows.*

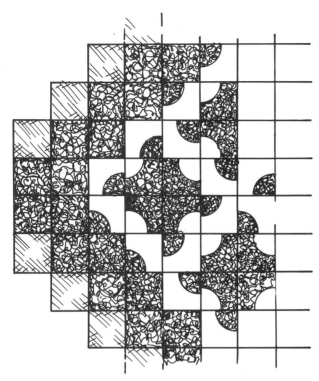

Fig. 1-5 *Stitch the rows together to form the quilt top.*

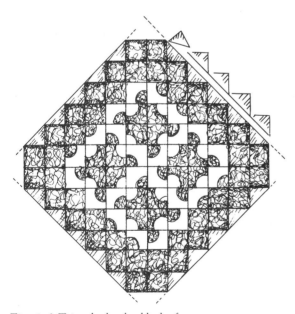

Fig. 1-6 *Trim the border blocks from corner to corner to form triangles.*

11. Put the quilt "sandwich" (quilt top, batting, backing) together and quilt. I quilted circles in the centers of the four squares created by the path. Between the path and the border I echo quilted the path. Bind the quilt with the extra border fabric.

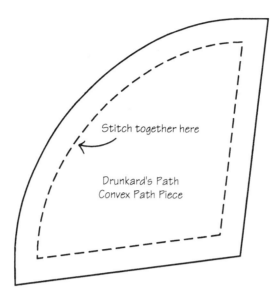

Stitch together here

Drunkard's Path
Convex Path Piece

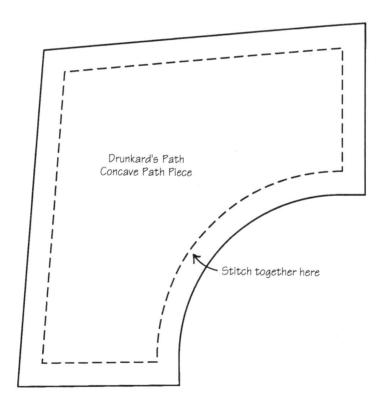

Drunkard's Path
Concave Path Piece

Stitch together here

Grandmother's Flower Garden

If the prospect of matching tricky corners has frightened you away from the Grandmother's Flower Garden quilt, you'll find that the three-dimensional version provides the freedom you've been looking for.

The fabric hexagons are basted to smaller muslin foundation hexa-

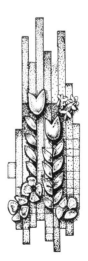

= "Flower" center hexagons

= "Flower" hexagons
(there are three other "flower"
fabrics shown)

= "Leaf" hexagons

Fig. 2-1 *Grandmother's Flower Garden*

gons, and their sides are tucked in to fit the shorter edges of the muslin pieces. This creates a puffed effect. The hexagons are then pieced together. No need for painstaking precision here; the puffiness of the pieced fabric hides any imperfect matches!

I used chintz prints for my quilt. To make the "flower" hexagons, I placed the large hexagon pattern (found at the end of this chapter) over the flowers on the fabric and marked around the pattern. For the green "leaf" hexagons, I placed the pattern over the leaves in the fabric. Don't worry if a little green gets in your purple or yellow seeps into the edges of your green hexagon: This is meant to be a "painterly" effect.

The amount of fabric you need depends on the effect you are trying to achieve and the print you are using. The density of the flowers in the fabric will determine the number of "flower" hexagons you can get out of it (and likewise for the leaves). You may want to go beyond the multiple colors in your fabric and buy another fabric to get a color you want. Mix and match fabrics so that you have purples, pinks, and peaches (or choose bolder colors).

By sewing together three-dimensional "flower" and "leaf" hexagons, you'll create the seven composite hexagons that make up the quilt (see Fig. 2-1). Think of all the quilt designs you could make three dimensional using this easy technique. For a nine patch of 2" (5 cm) squares, tuck the four edges of 3½" (9 cm) squares so that they match 2½" (6.5 cm) muslin squares. Piece the block as usual. You can make all the squares three dimensional or just the four corner squares and one center square. A single or double Irish Chain could be constructed in the same way.

The finished size of the Grandmother's Flower Garden quilt is 35" (89 cm) in diameter at its widest point.

Materials

¾ yard (.69 m) each of five or six fabrics (see chapter introduction for details of fabric selection)

Matching thread

2 yards (1.84 m) muslin

1¼ yards (1.15 m) backing fabric

Batting

Instructions

Note: *All seam allowances are* ¼″ *(6 mm) unless specified otherwise. Pattern pieces appear at the end of the chapter.*

1. Prepare the fabrics and patterns as instructed in "Fabric Preparation" and "How to Transfer Patterns" in The Basics.

2. Using the small hexagon pattern, cut 217 small hexagons from the muslin.

3. Using the large hexagon pattern and consulting Figure 1-1, cut large hexagons from the chintz fabrics as follows:

7 "flower" centers (color should contrast with surrounding "flowers")
18 "flower" hexagons for each of the seven flowers
84 green "leaf" hexagons

4. To make each three-dimensional "flower" hexagon, put together a large, chintz "flower" hexagon and one small muslin hexagon, wrong sides facing. Tuck one edge of the larger hexagon to match one edge of the smaller hexagon (see Fig. 2-2). Pin. Machine baste less than ¼″ (6 mm) from the raw edges. Repeat for the remaining sides of the hexagon. Repeat for all remaining hexagons, both "flowers" and "leaves."

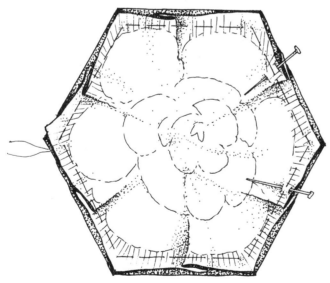

Fig. 2-2 *Placing the wrong side of the chintz against the wrong side of the muslin, make a tuck on one edge of a chintz piece until that edge matches the muslin edge. Pin. Repeat for all edges of the hexagon. Baste.*

5. To make one of the seven composite flowers in the quilt, match a 3-D "flower" hexagon to a 3-D "flower" center hexagon, right sides facing. Machine stitch one edge from dot to dot (Figs. 2-3a and b).

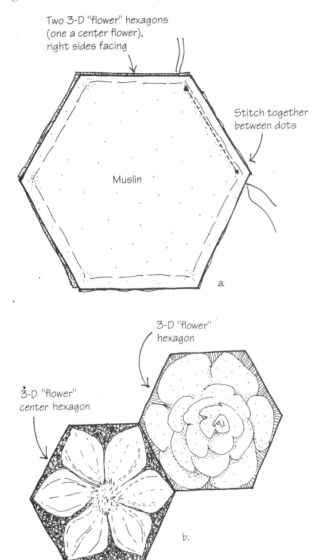

Two 3-D "flower" hexagons (one a center flower), right sides facing

Stitch together between dots

Muslin

a.

3-D "flower" hexagon

3-D "flower" center hexagon

b.

Fig. 2-3 With the right sides of the fabric facing match one straight edge of a 3-D "flower" center hexagon to one straight edge of a 3-D "flower" hexagon. Stitch from dot to dot.

6. Add another 3-D "flower" hexagon by stitching it, with right sides facing, to both the 3-D center hexagon and the first 3-D "flower" hexagon (Fig. 2-4a). Continue adding "flower" hexagons to complete the composite flower (Fig. 2-4b).

7. Piece the remaining six composite flowers.

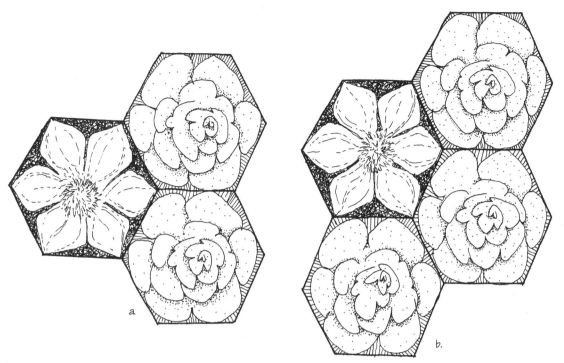

Fig. 2-4 *Add another 3-D "flower" hexagon, stitching one edge of the new hexagon to the 3-D "flower" center and an adjacent edge to the previous "flower" hexagon. Continue adding 3-D "flower" hexagons until you have six around the "flower" center hexagon. Then add another row of twelve 3-D "flower" hexagons.*

8. Lay out the seven composite flowers for the quilt top. Add a row of green "leaf" hexagons around the outside of the center flower (Fig. 2-5). This row of "leaves" will be part of each of the other six "leaf" rows (see color photograph and Fig. 2-1).

"Leaf" row

Fig. 2-5 *Add a row of green "leaf" hexagons to the outside edge of the center composite flower.*

9. Stitch a second composite flower to the "leaf" hexagons (Fig. 2-6). Continue in this manner until you have completed the quilt top. This is where the puffiness of the 3-D hexagons will help you hide any pieces that don't match up exactly, which is one of the virtues of 3-D piecing.

Fig. 2-6 *Add a second composite flower to the center composite flower.*

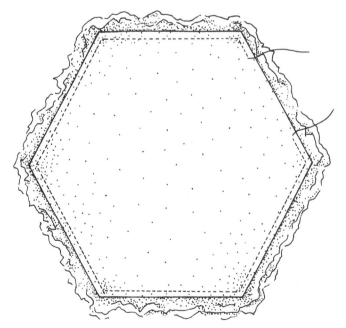

Fig. 2-7 *Stitch around the outside edge of the quilt, leaving a gap in the stitching along one edge for turning.*

10. Lay the batting on a large flat surface. Lay the backing right side up on top of the batting. Lay the quilt top right side down on top of the batting and backing. Pin the layers together, starting at the center and working around the edge. Trim away excess backing and batting to within a few inches of the edge of the quilt top. Stitch all the way around the edge of the quilt top, leaving an opening along one edge as shown in Figure 2-7.

11. Trim the backing and batting even with the edges of the quilt top. Clip into corners and trim off points (Fig. 2-8).

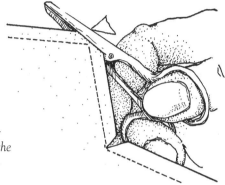

Fig. 2-8 *Trim away the seam allowances at all points. Clip into the seam allowances at all inside corners.*

12. Turn the quilt right side out. From inside the quilt, use a pointed object to push the edges of the quilt hexagons out cleanly. Ladderstitch the opening closed. Safety pin the three layers together. Quilt in the ditch around the individual hexagons.

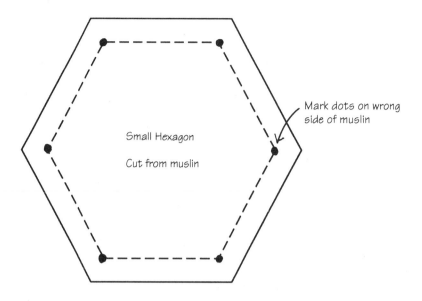

Small Hexagon

Cut from muslin

Mark dots on wrong side of muslin

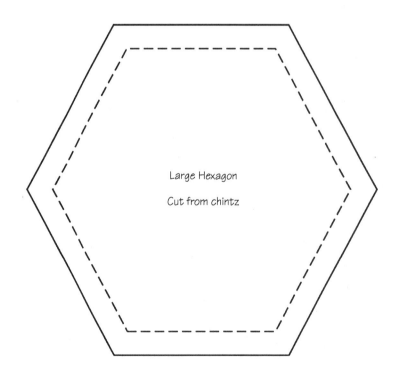

Large Hexagon

Cut from chintz

Kaleidoscope

3

A perfect candidate for a scrap quilt, the Kaleidoscope quilt is composed of hills and valleys, thanks to the raised centers of each kaleidoscope block. The inner yellow print border, or "frame," is also three dimensional, stuffed and inserted between the border and the quilt's pieced center.

Fig. 3-1 *Kaleidoscope*

The finished size of the Kaleidoscope quilt is 29″ (73.5 cm) square.

Materials

Assorted scraps for the kaleidoscope blocks
1 yard (.92 m) fabric (red) for border, background, and binding
¾ yard (.69 m) fabric (yellow print) for inner border, "frame", and kaleidoscope centers
1 yard (.92 m) backing fabric
Thread

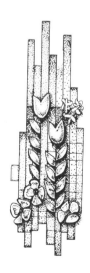

Polyester fiberfill stuffing
Batting

Instructions

Note: *All seam allowances are ¼″ (6 mm) unless specified otherwise. Patterns appear at the end of the chapter.*

1. Prepare fabrics and patterns as instructed in "Fabric Preparation" and "How to Transfer Patterns" in The Basics.

2. Using the kaleidoscope side pattern, cut 288 kaleidoscope side pieces from the fabric scraps.

3. Using the kaleidoscope center pattern, cut 36 center circles from the inner border fabric.

4. Using the background triangle pattern, cut 144 background corner triangles from the red background fabric.

5. For the "frame," cut four strips from the yellow inner border fabric, each 2½″ (6.5 cm) × 24½″ (62 cm).

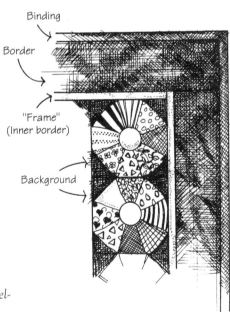

Fig. 3-2 *The Kaleidoscope quilt has a yellow inner border that "frames" it.*

6. From the border fabric, cut two short pieces, each 2½″ (6.5 cm) × 24½″ (62 cm), and two long pieces, each 2½″ (6.5 cm) × 28½″ (72 cm).

7. For each of the 36 blocks, stitch eight kaleidoscope side pieces together along their long, straight edges to form a ring (Fig. 3-3).

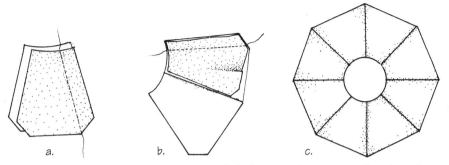

Fig. 3-3 *With right sides facing, stitch two kaleidoscope side pieces together along their straight side edges. Add six more pieces, for a total of eight. Join the first and last pieces to form a circle.*

8. With right sides facing, match a point on the edge of a center circle to a point along the inside edge of a kaleidoscope ring. Start stitching here (Fig. 3-4a). Match the edges of the center circle with those of the ring for about ½″ (1.3 cm) at a time. Stitch. Leaving the needle in the fabric, lift the presser foot and match another ½″ (1.3 cm) or so. Stitch. Continue until you have stitched the entire circle (Fig. 3-4b). Repeat for each kaleidoscope ring.

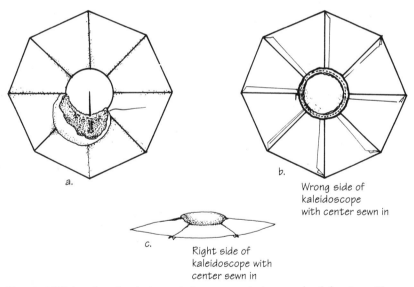

Wrong side of
kaleidoscope
with center sewn in

Right side of
kaleidoscope with
center sewn in

Fig. 3-4 *With right sides facing, stitch a center circle to each of the rings. You may have to stop to rearrange the fabric every ½″ (1.3 cm) or so.*

9. Stitch a background triangle piece to the outside edge of every other kaleidoscope side piece (Fig. 3-5). Press.

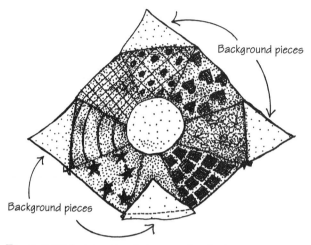

Fig. 3-5 *With right sides facing, stitch a background triangle to the outside edge of every other side piece.*

10. Stitch two completed kaleidoscope squares together, right sides facing. Open them up and add a third square (Fig. 3-6a). Add three more kaleidoscope pieces to make a strip of six (Fig. 3-6b). Repeat to make six strips.

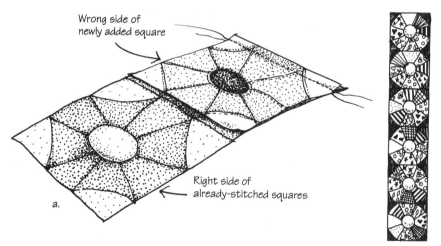

Fig. 3-6 *After stitching two kaleidoscope squares together, right sides facing, open them up and add another square. Continue to add squares until you have a strip of six.*

11. Lay the backing fabric down, wrong side up. Lay the batting on top. Lay a strip of kaleidoscope blocks along the left side of the backing/batting, right side up and 4″ (10 cm) or so from the edge. Stitch along the left-hand edge of the strip through all layers. Stuff each of the six kaleidoscope blocks lightly with fiberfill to give them shape. Lay a second strip of blocks *on top* of this first strip, right sides facing and raw edges even. Stitch along the right-hand edge through all layers, matching the horizontal seams (Fig. 3-7). (If the bulk of the quilt is troublesome, try using a zipper foot on your sewing machine.) Continue on in this manner until you have stuffed and stitched all of the strips.

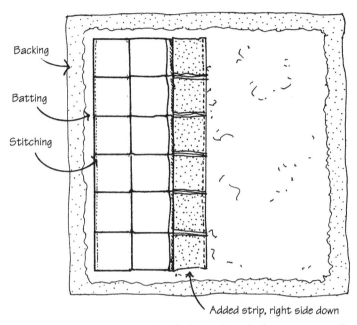

Backing

Batting

Stitching

Added strip, right side down

Fig. 3-7 *Lay the backing right side down. Lay the batting on top. Lay one strip, right side up, about 4" (10 cm) in from the left-hand edge of the batting and backing. Stitch along the left-hand edge through all layers. Stuff the first strip of blocks. Add another strip, right side down, on top of the first one, with the right-hand raw edges even. Stitch along the right-hand edge of the two strips through all layers, matching the horizontal seams. Fold the new strip over, stuff it lightly, and add another strip.*

12. With the quilt top right side up, topstitch horizontally along the sides of each block and along the top and bottom edges of the strips.

13. To make the "frame," fold one inner border piece in half along its long side, right sides facing. Stitch the short edges together on both ends (Fig. 3-8). Turn right side out. Press.

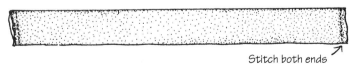

Stitch both ends

Fig. 3-8 *Fold an inner border piece in half lengthwise, right sides facing. On each end, stitch the short edges together.*

14. Cut a strip of batting 24″ (61 cm) long and a scant 1″ (2.5 cm) wide. Insert the batting into the inner border between the two layers. Baste the long straight edges of the inner border together (Fig. 3-9).

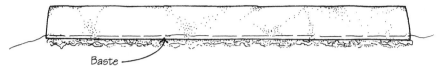

Baste

Fig. 3-9 *Insert the batting into the inner border piece between the two layers. Baste along the long edge.*

15. Repeat Steps 13 and 14 to make three more inner border strips.

16. Pin one inner border to the right side of one edge of the quilt. The inner border will be ½″ (1.3 cm) shorter than the quilt top. Leave ¼″ (6 mm) of quilt top on each end of the inner border. Baste (Fig. 3-10).

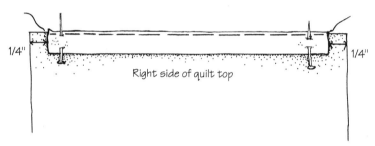

1/4″   1/4″

Right side of quilt top

Fig. 3-10 *Pin one inner border to the right side of one edge of the quilt top. Each end of the border should be ¼″ (6 mm) in from the end of the quilt top. Baste.*

Repeat for the remaining three edges of the quilt top.

17. Keeping the inner borders flat against the quilt top (i.e., do not open them out yet, but leave them as shown in Fig. 3-10), lay one short border piece face down along the left edge of the quilt top. The raw edges of the border, inner border, and quilt top should all be even. Place the other short border piece along the opposite edge of the quilt top in a similar fashion. Stitch through all layers on both border edges. When you open up the two short borders, the inner borders should stand up perpendicular to the quilt top, forming a "frame" for the quilt. To retain the "frame" effect, press the outer borders only (Fig. 3-11).

18. Repeat Step 17 for the two long border pieces, stitching them to the two remaining edges of the quilt top as shown in Figure 3-12.

19. Trim the batting and backing even with the outside edges of the quilt (including border fabric). Quilt the border if desired. Bind the quilt.

Short border piece

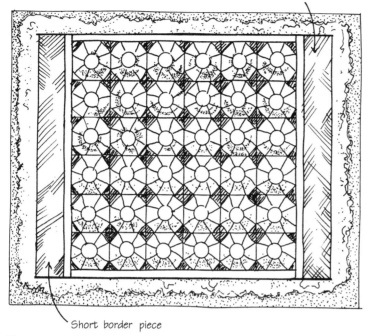

Short border piece

Fig. 3-11 *With right sides facing, stitch a short border piece to one side of the quilt top. Stitch the remaining short border piece to the opposite edge of the quilt.*

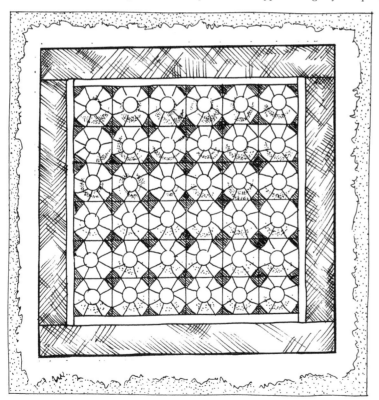

Fig. 3-12 *With right sides facing, stitch the two long border pieces to the two remaining edges of the quilt top.*

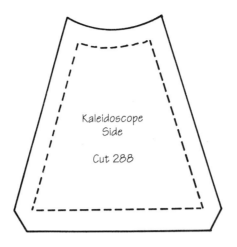

Kaleidoscope
Side

Cut 288

Kaleidoscope
Center

Cut 36

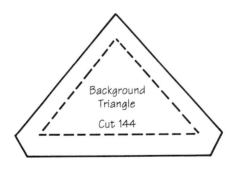

Background
Triangle

Cut 144

Double Wedding Ring

4

By simply enlarging the rings and gathering them, you can create a Double Wedding Ring quilt that has a puffy appearance and is easy to piece.

Though I chose silver and gold lamé, bridal satin, and lace, you might prefer traditional calicos or designer cottons. They all will produce an exciting quilt. A black background with jewel-colored rings is a sure winner.

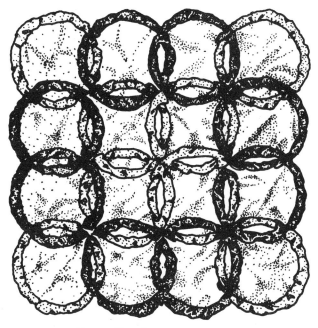

Fig. 4-1 *Double Wedding Ring*

The finished size of the Double Wedding Ring quilt is 33″ (84 cm) square.

Materials

2 yards (1.84 m) each of two ring fabrics (I used silver and gold lamé)

4 yards (3.68 m) knit fusible interfacing if using lamé

1½ yards (1.38 m) background fabric (Bridal satin can be used, with or without lace)

1½ yards (1.38 m) lace fabric (optional)

1¼ yards (1.15 m) backing fabric

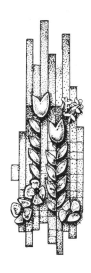

Fabric glue stick (if using lace fabric)
Matching thread
Batting

Instructions

Note: All seam allowances are ¼″ (6 mm) unless specified otherwise. Patterns appear at the end of the chapter.

1. Prepare the fabrics and patterns as instructed in "Fabric Preparation" and "How to Transfer Patterns" in The Basics.

2. If using lamé, fuse the interfacing to the wrong side of the lamé.

3. Using the patterns you created in Step 1, trace and cut 20 small and 4 large silver ring pieces, 4 small and 28 large gold ring pieces, and 4 silver corner edge ring pieces. Trace onto the wrong side of the fabric or the interfacing if using lamé.

4. From the background fabric cut the following:

4 of background piece A
8 of background piece B
4 of background piece C
24 of the pointed oval piece D

5. If you are making the background out of bridal satin *and* lace fabric, cut the satin according to Step 4. For the lace fabric, follow Step 4 but cut background pieces A, B, and C and pointed oval piece D slightly larger than the satin pieces. To adhere the lace to the satin, center each lace piece, right side up, on top of the matching satin piece (also right side up) and tack the wrong side of the lace to the right side of the satin with a few dabs of fabric glue stick.

6. Start by creating one of the four center rings. To assemble each ring, the pointed ovals that occur where two rings overlap (see Fig. 4-1) must be sewn first. To assemble the first oval, oval 1, gather stitch along the inside curved edge of one small silver ring piece. Pull up on the gather stitches to match one edge of the pointed oval piece D. Pin the ring piece to the oval piece, right sides facing, and stitch (Fig. 4-2).

7. Gather stitch along the inside edge of one large gold ring piece. Pull up on the gather stitches; match to other side of oval 1, right sides facing; pin; stitch to the pointed oval piece and the ends of the small ring piece (Fig. 4-3).

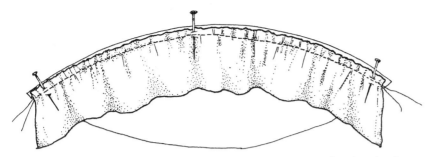

Fig. 4-2 *Gather the inside curve of a short silver ring piece. With right sides facing, pin it to an oval background piece. Pull up on the gather stitches to fit. Stitch.*

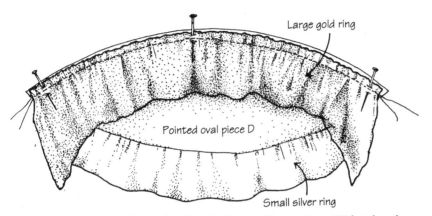

Large gold ring

Pointed oval piece D

Small silver ring

Fig. 4-3 *Gather along the inside edge of a large gold ring piece. With right sides facing, pin to the other side of the oval and the ends of the small ring. Pull up on and adjust the gather stitches to fit. Pin. Stitch.*

Designing as a Way of Life

Designing used to take a lot of mental and emotional effort for me, and often kept me from sleeping. Now it turns off with my worklight at midnight, and is back with me and ready to go in the morning. It is a natural part of me, and I'm at ease with it.

One of the smartest things I've done for designing is put up a flannel sheet on the wall at the foot of our bed. The last thing I see at night and the first thing I see when I awaken is the quilt in process on my "design wall." At night, in low light, a piece of fabric may jump out at me and tell me it doesn't work, thus revealing a problem I couldn't see under the brighter lights of the work day.

8. Repeat Steps 6 and 7 to create oval 2. To make ovals 3 and 4, use a small silver and a large silver ring piece.

9. Gather stitch along the outside edge of the large gold ring piece of oval 1. Take one background piece A and fold it to find its center along one edge. Do the same with the outside gold edge of oval 1 (Figs. 4-4a and b). Pin center to center, right sides facing. Match and pin ends. Pull up on the gather stitches on the ring to match (Fig. 4-4c). Adjust the gathers. Pin. Stitch.

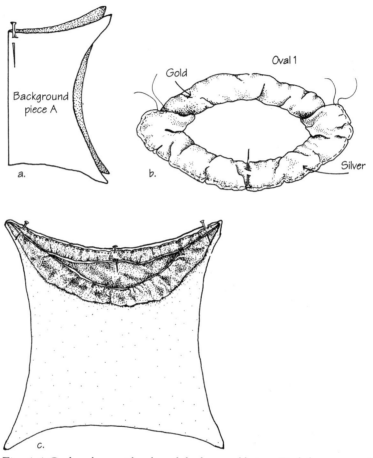

Fig. 4-4 *Gather the outside edge of the large gold ring. Find the centers of the gold ring and a background piece A and mark them with pins. Match and pin together the centers and the ends of the two pieces. Pull up on the gather stitches to fit. Stitch.*

10. Repeat Step 9 for oval 2, attaching it to an adjoining side of the background piece (Fig. 4-5). Do the same for ovals 3 and 4, gathering along the long silver edges and then attaching them to the remaining sides of background piece A.

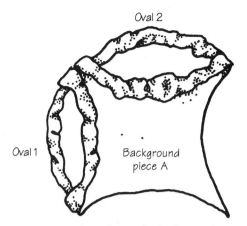

Fig. 4-5 *Stitch oval 2 to the background piece as you did for oval 1.*

11. Add a second background piece A to the outside silver piece of oval 3 (Fig. 4-6).

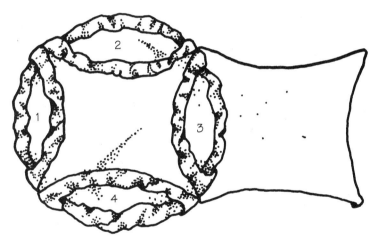

Fig. 4-6 *Stitch the second background piece A to the outside edge of the silver piece of oval 3.*

12. Make three more ovals (1, 2, and 4) for the second background piece; gather and stitch them in place (Fig. 4-7).

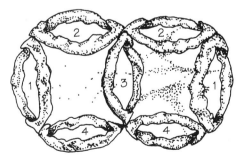

Fig. 4-7 *Prepare the ovals for the second background piece. Stitch them in place.*

13. Consulting the color photo of the quilt for oval placement, continue until you have the four background pieces A and their surrounding ovals in place. You have just made the four center rings. Now, using the gathering method explained in Step 9, add a background piece B to each of the eight outside ring pieces. Add the appropriate oval pieces on the sides of each background piece B (Fig. 4-8).

Fig. 4-8 *Continue building the quilt until you have all of the center background pieces and their adjacent ovals stitched in place.*

14. Using the gathering method from Step 9, add the corner background pieces C (Fig. 4-9).

15. Gather stitch the inside edge of eight large gold and four large silver corner edge ring pieces. Using the gathering method from Step 9, add the gold rings to the outside edges of the background pieces B and the silver corner edge ring pieces to the background pieces C (see Fig. 4-1).

16. Stitch the short ends of adjacent ring pieces together all the way around the quilt.

17. Gather stitch each of the ring pieces along their outside edges, all the way around the quilt.

18. Draw a 34" (86.5 cm) square on the right side of the quilt backing fabric. Cut a few inches (2–10 cm) outside of the marked lines. Line up the outside edge templates 1 and 2 inside the marked square, butting their edges against one another as shown in Figure 4-10. Trace their curved edges onto the fabric.

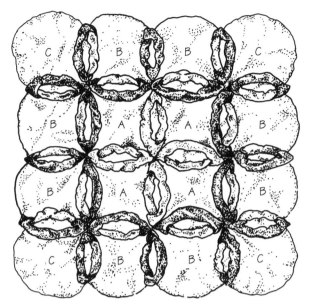

Fig. 4-9 *Stitch the corner pieces C to the ovals/rings.*

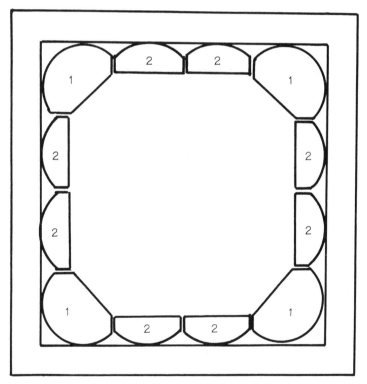

Fig. 4-10 *Line up outside edge templates 1 and 2, butting them up inside the marked square. Trace their curved edges.*

19. Lay the batting on a smooth surface. Lay the backing on top, right side up. Lay the quilt top, right side down, on top of both. Match the edges of the quilt top to the curved lines marked on the backing. Pull up on the gather stitches of each outside ring so that the quilt top fits within the marked lines. Pin. Stitch along the outside curved edge through all layers, leaving an opening for turning (Fig. 4-11).

Fig. 4-11 *Lay down the backing right side up. Lay the quilt top right side down on top. Pin. Stitch, leaving an opening for turning.*

20. Trim the backing and batting to ¼″ (6 mm). If using bridal satin, apply Fray Check to the raw edges, especially at the opening. Turn the quilt right side out. Hand stitch the opening closed. Lay the quilt right side up on a flat surface. Adjust the quilt top so that the ovals are arranged evenly. Pin baste. Quilt in the ditch along the seams of the rings.

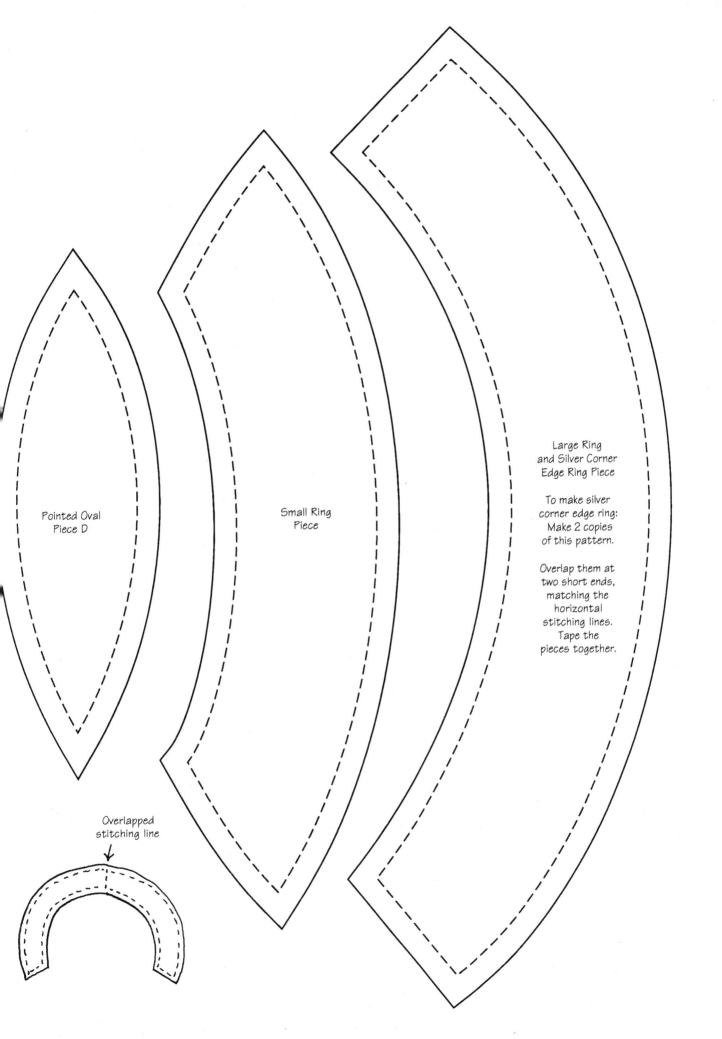

Pointed Oval
Piece D

Small Ring
Piece

Large Ring
and Silver Corner
Edge Ring Piece

To make silver
corner edge ring:
Make 2 copies
of this pattern.

Overlap them at
two short ends,
matching the
horizontal
stitching lines.
Tape the
pieces together.

Overlapped
stitching line

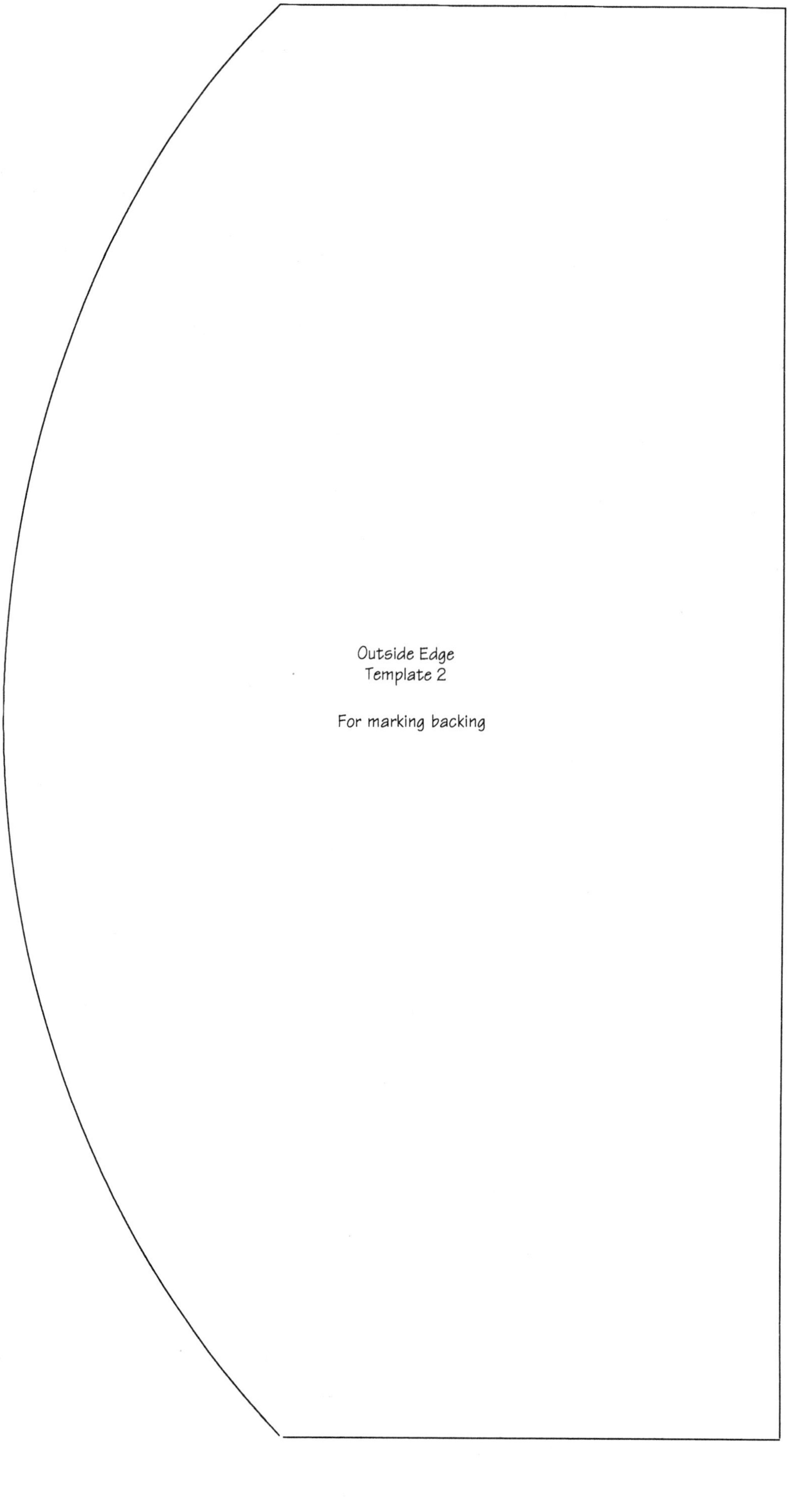

Outside Edge
Template 2

For marking backing

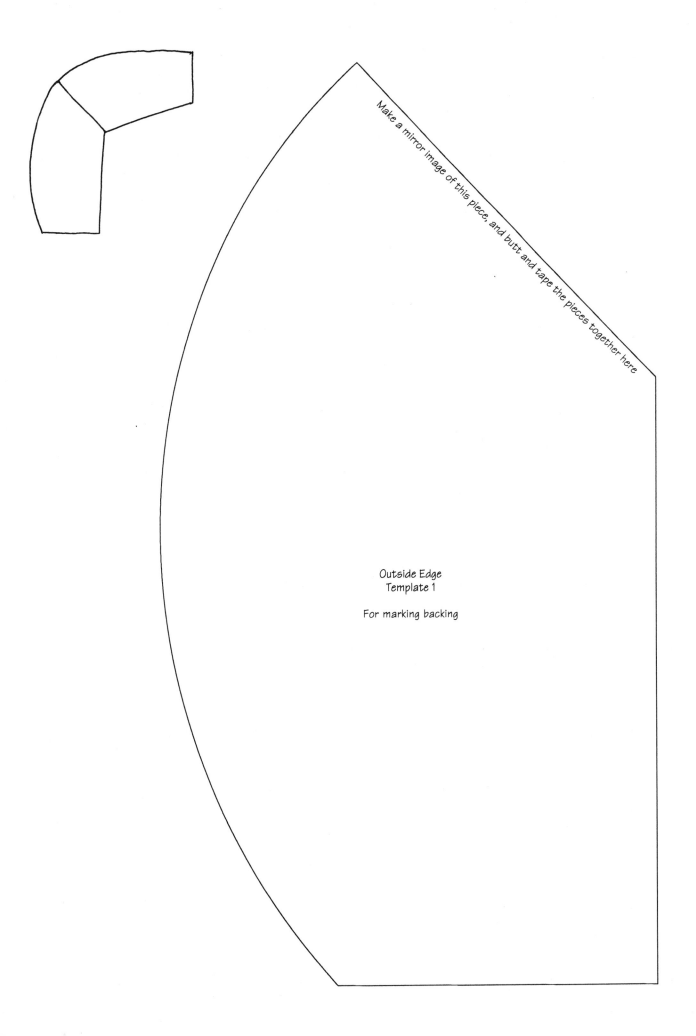

Make a mirror image of this piece, and butt and tape the pieces together here

Outside Edge
Template 1

For marking backing

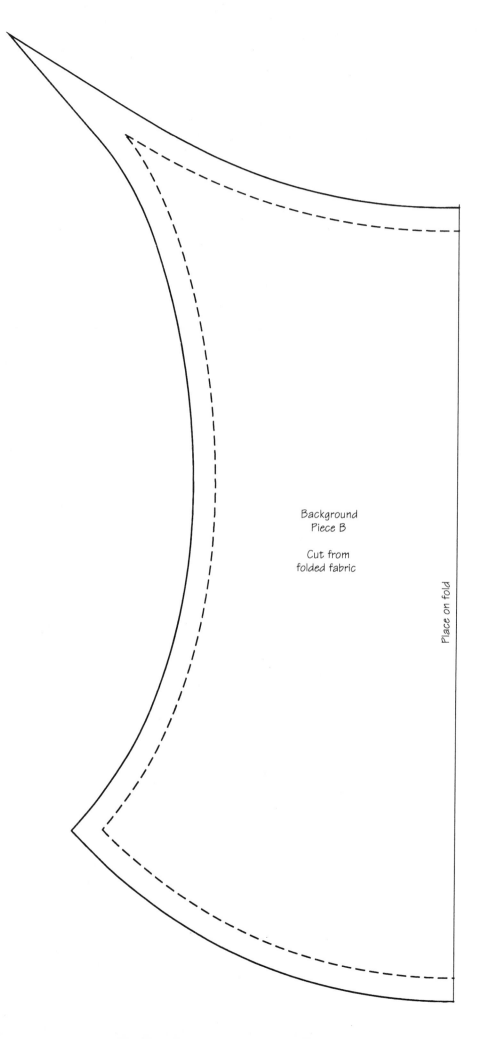

Background
Piece B

Cut from
folded fabric

Place on fold

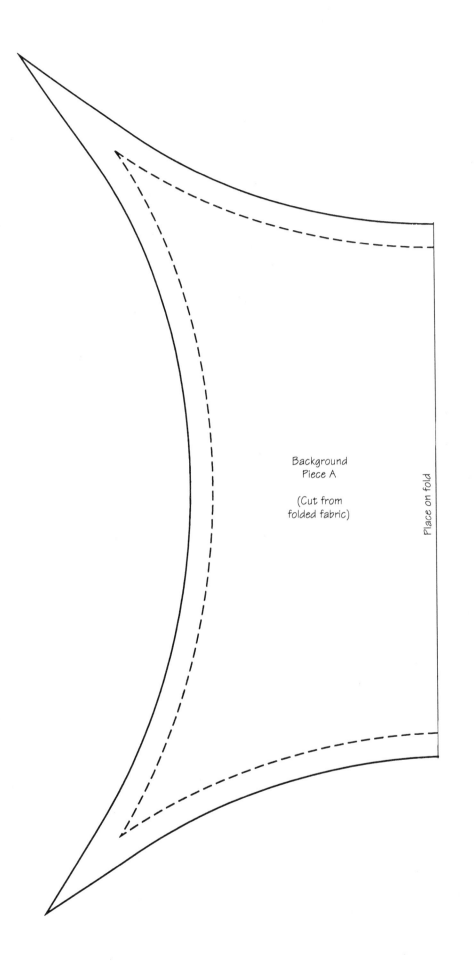

Background
Piece A

(Cut from
folded fabric)

Place on fold

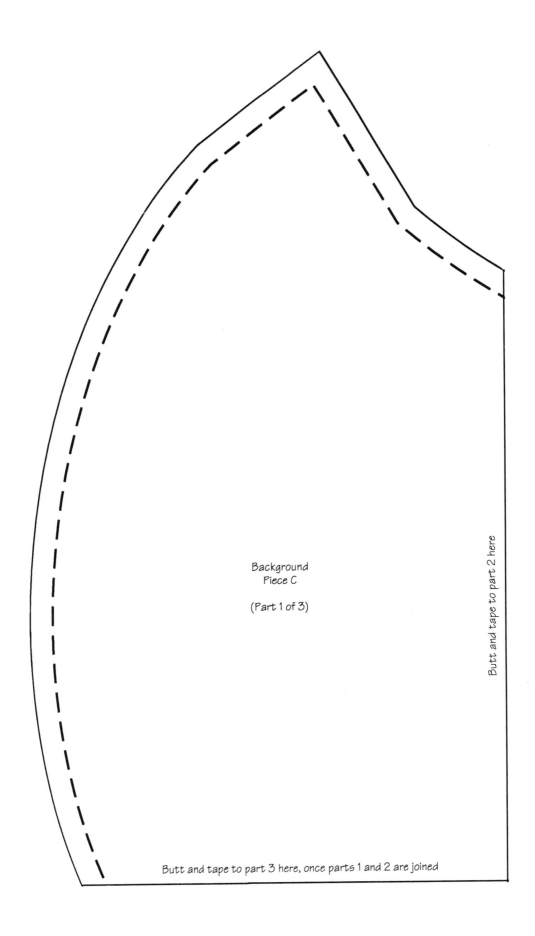

Background
Piece C

(Part 1 of 3)

Butt and tape to part 2 here

Butt and tape to part 3 here, once parts 1 and 2 are joined

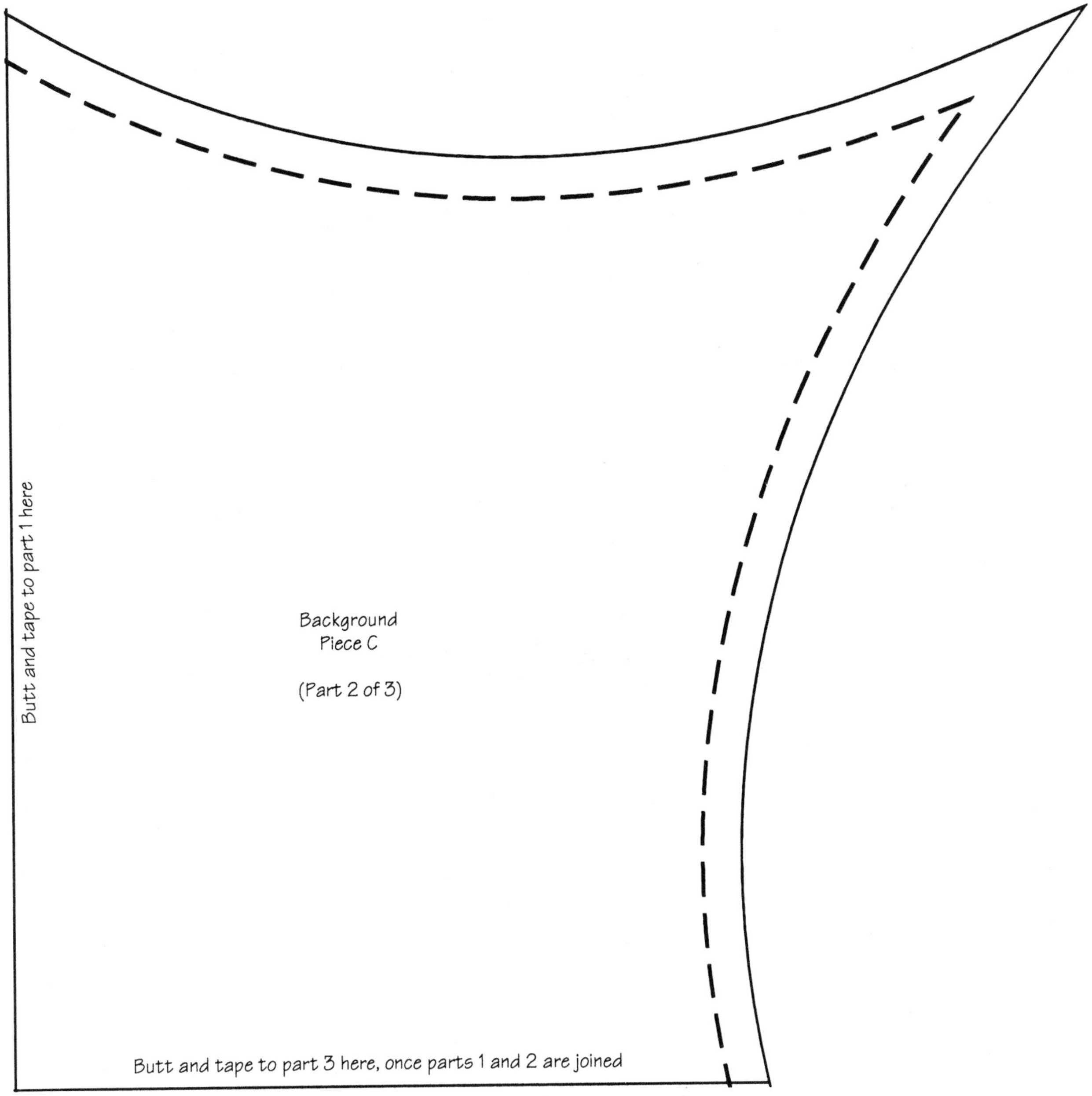

Butt and tape to part 1 here

Background
Piece C

(Part 2 of 3)

Butt and tape to part 3 here, once parts 1 and 2 are joined

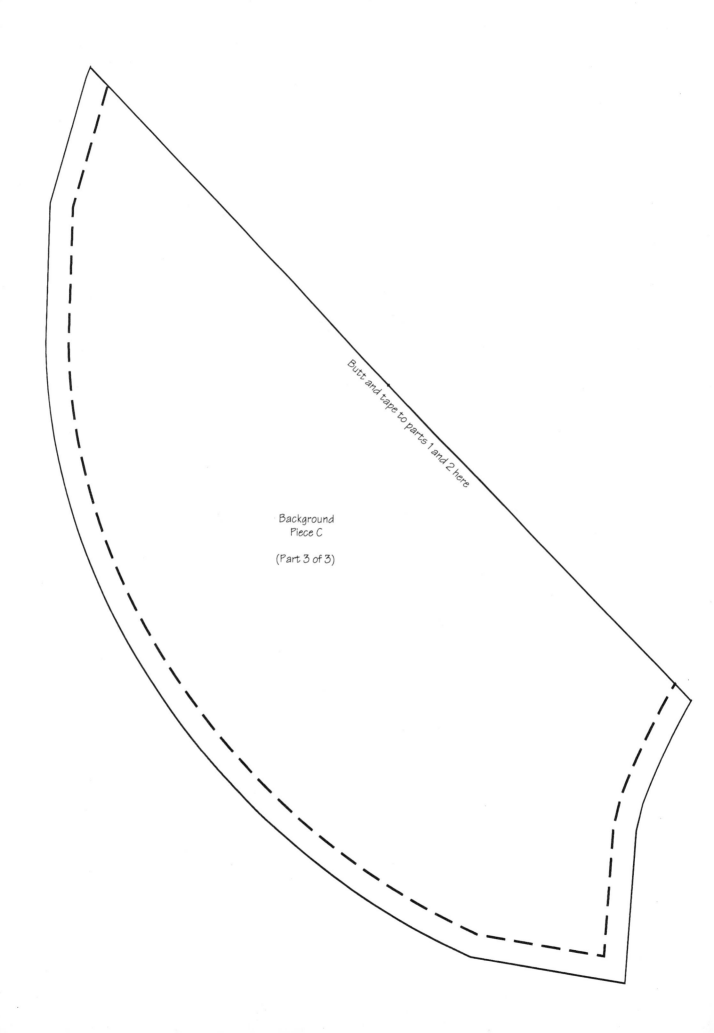

Butt and tape to parts 1 and 2 here

Background
Piece C

(Part 3 of 3)

Three-Dimensional
Variations on Tradition

Love Puzzle

5

Based on the Love Ring variation of Drunkard's Path, this quilt is an excellent beginner's project. The "path" (see Fig. 5-1) is gathered to the flat pieces. No need to worry about tucks and other piecing mistakes—the gathers will hide them!

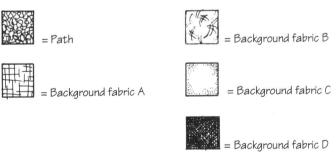

= Path

= Background fabric B

= Background fabric A

= Background fabric C

= Background fabric D

Fig. 5-1 *Love Puzzle*

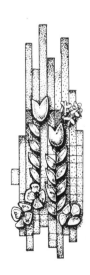

Rather than use four background fabrics as I did, you may wish to use two, one for the gathered path (the print in the color photo) and a second fabric for the flat background.

The finished size of the Love Puzzle quilt is 48″ (122 cm) square.

Materials

2¼ yards (2.07 m) fabric for gathered "path" and binding
¼ yard (.23 m) background fabric A
⅓ yard (30.5 cm) background fabric B
⅞ yard (.80 m) background fabric C
⅝ yard (.57 m) background fabric D
3 yards (2.76 m) backing fabric
Matching thread
Batting

Instructions

Note: All seam allowances are ¼″ (6 mm) unless specified otherwise. Patterns appear at the end of the chapter.

1. Prepare the fabrics and patterns as instructed in "Fabric Preparation" and "How to Transfer Patterns" in The Basics.

2. Using the patterns you prepared in Step 1, cut the background fabrics A, B, C, D, and the path fabric according to the cutting chart.

Love Puzzle Cutting Chart

	Number of Pieces to Cut			
Fabric	*Background Piece I*	*Background Piece II*	*Path Piece I*	*Path Piece II*
Background fabric A	8	4		
Background fabric B	8	12		
Background fabric C	32	32		
Background fabric D	24	24		
Path fabric			72	72

3. Gather stitch the curved edge of all of the path pieces (Fig. 5-2).

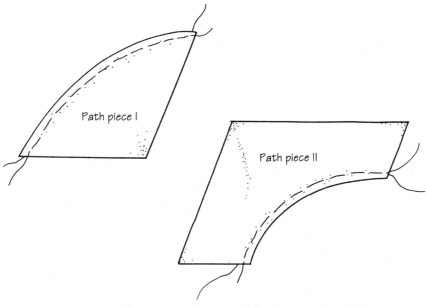

Fig. 5-2 *Gather stitch along the curved edges of all path pieces I and II.*

4. Find the centers of the path pieces and background pieces by folding the pieces in half along their curved edges (Fig. 5-3).

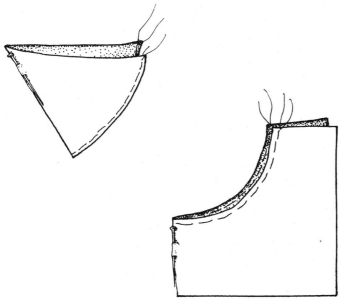

Fig. 5-3 *To find the centers of the background and path pieces, fold the pieces in half and mark the fold with a pin.*

5. Match and pin the centers of each path piece I to a background piece II and each path piece II to a background piece I along their curved edges, right sides facing. Match and pin the corner edges. Pull up on the gather stitches to fit (Fig. 5-4). Pin. Stitch. Press the seam allowances toward the path pieces.

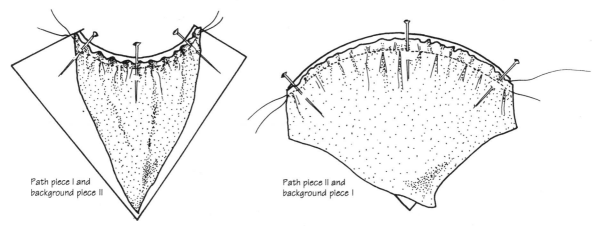

Path piece I and background piece II

Path piece II and background piece I

Fig. 5-4 *With right sides facing, match and pin the centers of path piece I to background piece II and path piece II to background piece I. Match and pin the corner edges.*

The Creative Flow

I've been designing for so long that the ideas flow freely, quickly, and the process of making them happen runs smoothly. But it wasn't always that way.

In my early attempts I'd get so frustrated when I couldn't figure out what to do next or things weren't working that I'd trash the idea and the uncompleted project with it. Sometimes this is the thing to do, but more often the "ah yes!" inspiration simply hasn't come yet. Now I know to be patient (even with looming deadlines) and not to worry. I set the project aside and work on something else.

Also, I get opinions. A look through a fresh pair of eyes, even those of a non-quilter, might pick out what isn't obvious to me. Often what's needed is a new perspective, not a completely new idea.

6. Follow the diagram in Figure 5-1 to lay out the pieced blocks that form the quilt top. Starting at the top right-hand corner, stitch the blocks into vertical rows (Fig. 5-5).

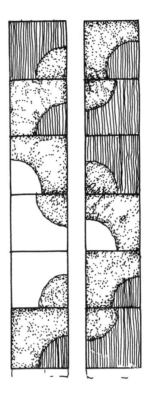

Fig. 5-5 *Stitch the blocks into vertical rows.*

7. For the first row, press the seam allowances up. For the second row press them down, for the third row up, and so forth. Matching seams, stitch the first row to the second row. Stitch the third row to the second row. Continue in this manner until the quilt top is completed. Press the seam allowances to one side.

8. Cut the backing fabric into two 1½-yard (1.38 m) lengths. Remove the selvages. With right sides facing, match one long edge of each piece. Stitch. Press.

9. Put the quilt "sandwich" (quilt top, batting, and backing) together and quilt. I echo quilted around the path pieces and quilted along the seams between the background pieces, but instead of stitching straight along straight lines, I bowed them out about ⅜" (1 cm) at the centers for a more interesting effect. Finally, bind the quilt.

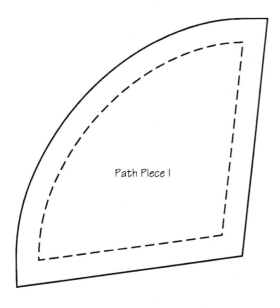

Path Piece I

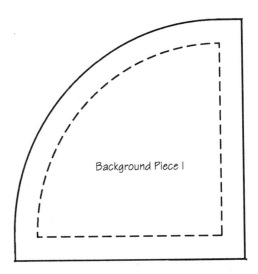

Background Piece I

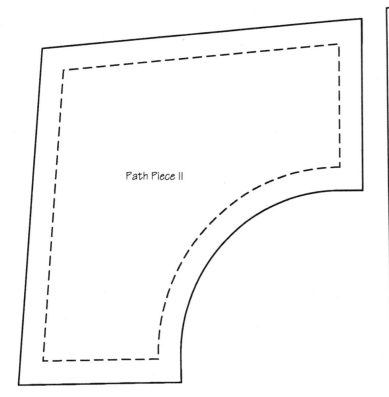

Path Piece II

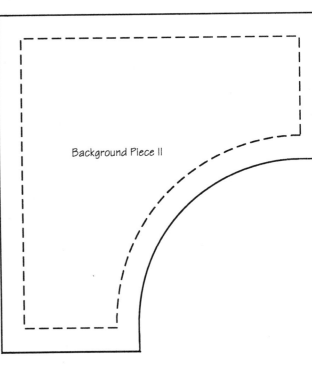

Background Piece II

Lone Star

6

This Lone Star quilt is the result of an experiment I did while working on my previous book on three-dimensional quilting, *Three-Dimensional Appliqué*.

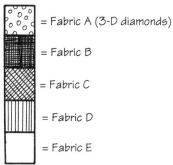

= Fabric A (3-D diamonds)

= Fabric B

= Fabric C

= Fabric D

= Fabric E

Fig. 6-1 *Lone Star*

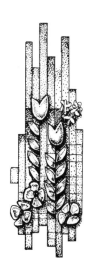

In trying out an idea of appliquéing stuffed diamonds to create a Lone Star, I decided the idea would be best pieced. Aha! Three-dimensional piecing, I thought. That's another book!

And here it is.

On paper I figured I would make every diamond three dimensional. A friend wisely suggested that the effect would be lost if I did so, not to mention that it would be a lot of work. Instead, each ray of this Lone Star has a center row of stuffed diamonds that rise in peaks from the quilt top. These diamonds are made of four pieces, much like faceted jewels. The remaining diamonds lie flat in the traditional manner.

The finished size of the Lone Star quilt is 52″ (132 cm) square.

Materials

1 yard (.92 m) fabric A
1 yard (.92 m) fabric B
1 yard (.92 m) fabric C
1 yard (.92 m) fabric D
½ yard (.46 m) fabric E
1 yard (.92 m) muslin
1½ yards (1.38 m) background fabric
3¼ yards (2.76 m) backing fabric
Matching thread
Polyester fiberfill stuffing
Batting
½ yard (.46 m) fabric for binding

Instructions

Note: All seam allowances are ¼″ (6 mm) unless specified otherwise. Patterns appear at the end of the chapter.

1. Prepare the fabrics and patterns as instructed in "Fabric Preparation" and "How to Transfer Patterns" in The Basics.

2. Using the diamond foundation pattern cut 40 diamonds from the muslin. These will be the backing for the three-dimensional diamonds.

Garden at Dusk
38" (96.5 cm) x 28" (71 cm)
Chapter Twelve

Pocket Drunkard's Path
29" (73.5 cm) square
Chapter One

Love Puzzle
48" (122 cm) square
Chapter Five

3. Using the diamond pattern, cut diamonds as follows:

- From fabric B, cut 48
- From fabric C, cut 48
- From fabric D, cut 48
- From fabric E, cut 16

4. For the background, cut four 16″ (40.5 cm) squares from the background fabric with their edges on the crosswise and lengthwise grain of the fabric. Cut two more 16″ (40.5 cm) squares from the background fabric with their edges on the bias of the fabric (Fig. 6-2a). Cut these two bias-cut squares in half diagonally to make the background triangles (Fig. 6-2b).

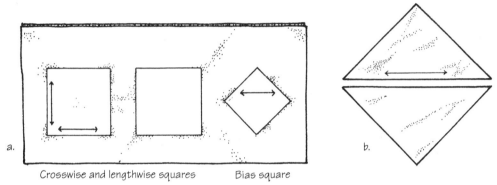

Crosswise and lengthwise squares   Bias square

Fig. 6-2 *Cut the background squares. Take each square cut on the bias and cut it in half across its diagonal center.*

The Power of Play

For beginning designers who have no idea where to start but have plenty of desire, I suggest beginning with a traditional quilt block. Play with it, change a line, reposition elements. Couple it with another block. Get out your graph paper and colored pencils and play. Better yet, use a computer quilt-design program. Talk about fun! Instantaneous renditions of variations on your design idea appear magically on the screen.

Don't get hung up worrying about originality. There are no original ideas out there—just repackaging and manipulation. While I was working on the Flower Basket quilt idea for this book, a new quilting catalog arrived in the mail. On the back cover was a photo of a pattern for a quilt with loose triangles sewn into the seams, just like those in my design!

5. In making each half of the three-dimensional diamonds, I found it easiest to mark the diamonds on the fabric and stitch the first seam before cutting them out. To do so, fold fabric A in half so that the right sides are together. Take the 3-D diamond quarter pattern and trim it along the dashed center seam line (Fig. 6-3).

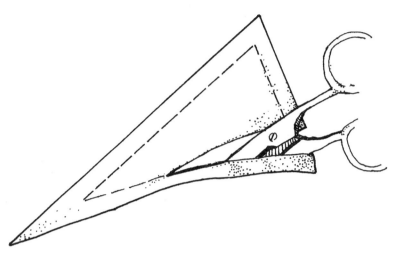

Fig. 6-3 *Trim the three-dimensional diamond quarter pattern along its center seam.*

6. Using your trimmed pattern (see Step 5), trace 80 three-dimensional diamonds on the wrong side of the folded fabric, marking each center seam as a dashed line. Stitch along each marked center seam line (Fig. 6-4). These seams will run vertically down the center of the finished diamonds. To make it easier to maneuver the fabric at the sewing machine, mark and stitch these in four batches.

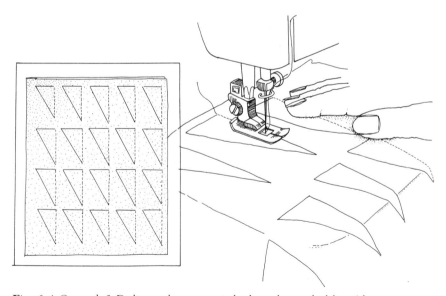

Fig. 6-4 *On each 3-D diamond quarter stitch along the marked line (the center seam line) through both layers of fabric.*

7. Cut out the 3-D diamond pieces by cutting just inside the marked lines on the two unstitched edges and ⅛″ (3 mm) outside the stitched line. Finger press the center seam open. You now have half of a diamond. Match the seams of two pieced halves, right sides together, and stitch as shown in Figure 6-5. Trim this seam to about ⅛″ (3 mm). Finger press to one side. Repeat with remaining 3-D diamonds to make 40 pieces.

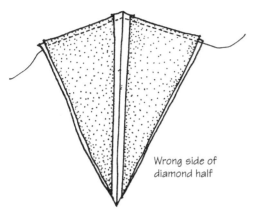

Wrong side of
diamond half

Fig. 6-5 *With right sides facing, match the seams of two pieced three-dimensional diamond halves. Stitch. Trim the seam allowance to ⅛″ (3 mm).*

A Holistic View

As for perfection, if that were my aim, I'd never finish anything. There's always more I could do, something I could change, but at some point I have to call the project finished and get on to the next one. I've learned to accept this feeling of never being satisfied as constructive. It spurs me on to grow with my creations. The alternative is stagnation.

Designing a quilt or anything else is not just a beginning and ending in itself, but a continual process from quilt to quilt to doll to quilt. Each piece teaches me something. Even planning the layout of my garden and decorating my house add to my growth. Each experience augments my design skills and my way of seeing. And with each project, I gain confidence in my ability to explore new territory and take new risks to bring my visions to life.

8. Baste a pieced 3-D diamond, wrong side down, to a muslin diamond (Fig. 6-6a). Being careful to cut through only one layer of fabric, make a small cut in the muslin back of the diamond to allow for stuffing later (Fig. 6-6b). Baste the remaining pieced 3-D diamonds to muslin diamonds and slit the muslin backs.

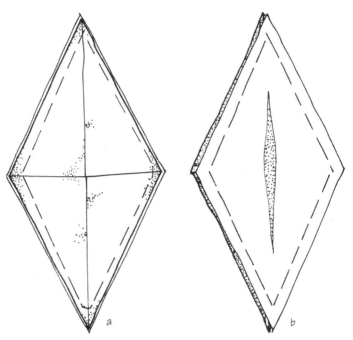

Fig. 6-6 *Place the wrong side of a pieced three-dimensional diamond face down on a muslin diamond and baste the four edges of the diamond to the muslin. Cut a slash in the muslin at the back of each three-dimensional diamond.*

9. Lay out one large diamond ray by arranging the diamonds cut out in Step 3 and the 3-D diamonds following the quilt diagram in Figure 6-1. Piece the diamonds into strips of five (Fig. 6-7).

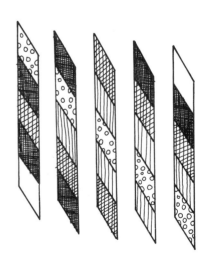

Fig. 6-7 *Lay out one of the eight rays. Piece five diamonds into each strip.*

10. Lay the five strips out in the large diamond shape. Press the seam allowances of the first strip up. Press the seam allowances of the second strip down, and so forth. Stitch the strips together, carefully matching seams, to form the large diamond ray. Repeat for the other seven large diamond rays of the Lone Star.

11. Stitch two large diamond rays together, stopping ¼″ (6 mm) from each end (Fig. 6-8). Repeat until you have four sets of two diamond rays each. Stitch two sets together along one edge, leaving ¼″ (6 mm) at the beginning and end of the stitching (Fig. 6-9). Repeat for the other two sets.

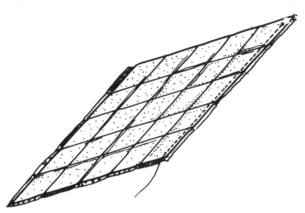

Fig. 6-8 *With their right sides facing, stitch two large diamond rays together.*

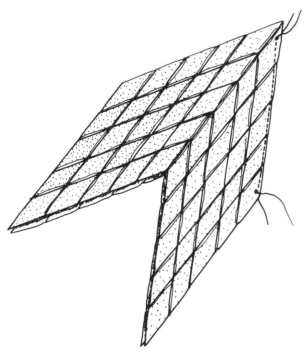

Fig. 6-9 *Stitch two pairs of large diamond rays together along one edge to form half of the Lone Star.*

12. Stitch the two halves of the Lone Star together, matching all seams and leaving ¼″ (6 mm) at the beginning and end of the stitching (Fig. 6-10). Press. To reduce bulk at the center, trim the seam allowances to approximately ⅛″ (3 mm).

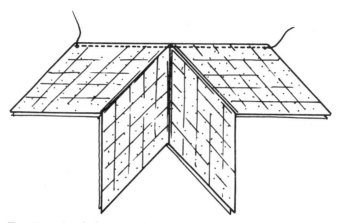

Fig. 6-10 *Stitch the two halves of the Lone Star together.*

13. For the corners of the quilt, stitch one edge of one background square to one edge of a diamond ray, right sides facing, as shown in Figure 6-11. Stitch the adjacent edge of the background square to the edge of the adjacent diamond. Repeat for the remaining three corners of the Lone Star.

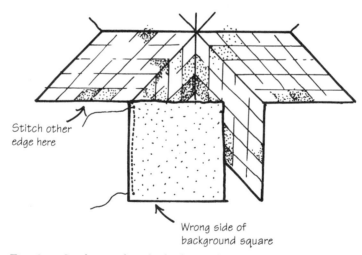

Stitch other edge here

Wrong side of background square

Fig. 6-11 *Stitch one edge of a background square to one of the large diamonds, right sides facing. This will be a corner of the quilt.*

14. Stitch one short side of one background triangle to one edge of a large diamond, right sides facing (Fig. 6-12a). Repeat for the other edge of the triangle. Do the same for the three remaining background triangles. Press. Trim excess from the outside edges of the background triangles to square up the quilt if necessary (Fig. 6-12b).

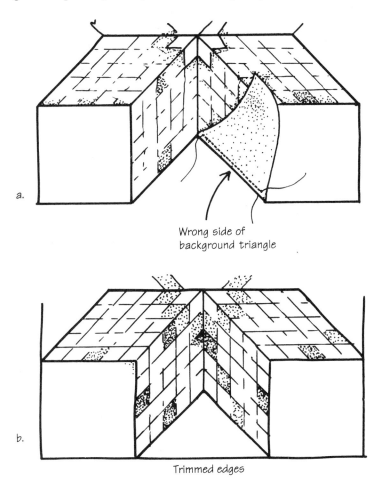

a.

Wrong side of
background triangle

b.

Trimmed edges

Fig. 6-12 *Stitch one side of one background triangle to one edge of a large diamond. Then stitch the next edge of the triangle to the adjacent large diamond.*

15. Softly stuff the three-dimensional diamonds with just enough fiberfill for them to hold their shape. Whipstitch the slashes in the muslin diamond backs closed.

16. Cut the backing fabric into two 1⅝-yard lengths. Remove the selvages. With right sides facing, match a long edge from each of the two pieces and stitch them together. Press the seam open.

17. Layer the quilt top, batting, and backing. Quilt. The quilt in the color section was quilted in the ditch along the seam lines of all but the three-dimensional diamonds. There are also stipple-quilted stars surrounded by swirls in the background squares and triangles. Bind the quilt.

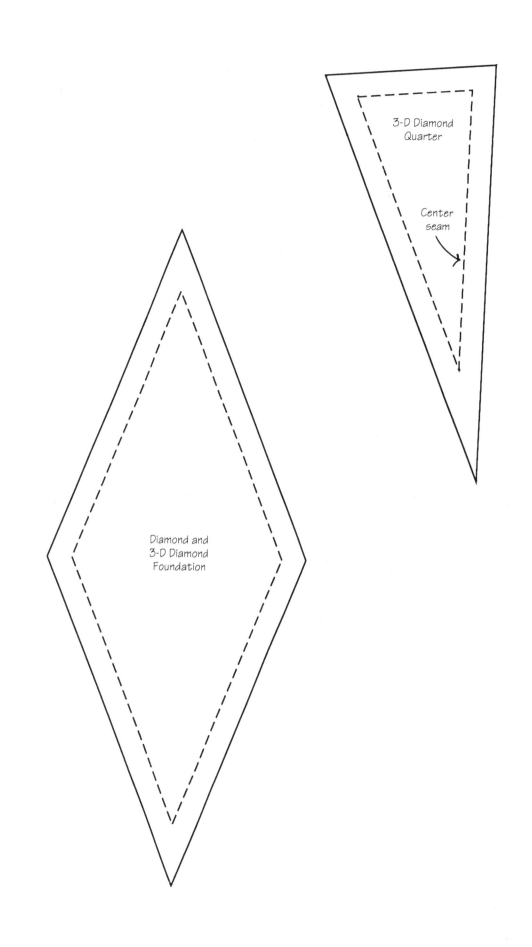

3-D Diamond
Quarter

Center
seam

Diamond and
3-D Diamond
Foundation

Swirling Fans

These three-dimensional pieced fans are larger than the blocks they are sewn to, causing them to ripple across the quilt top. Together with the graceful curves created by the positioning of the fans and the subtle shades of the lovely hand-dyed fabrics, the arched fans bring dimension to the tried-and-true Grandmother's Fan pattern.

For the backside (lining) of the fans, I chose the same fabric I used for the quilt top, rather than using the exquisite hand-dyed fabric where it wouldn't be seen.

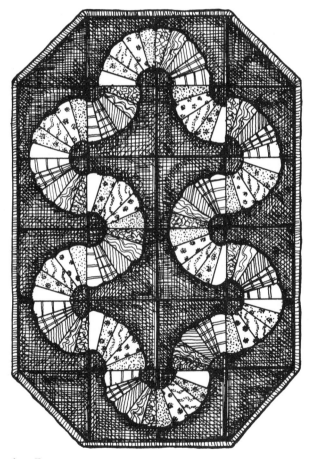

Fig. 7-1 *Swirling Fans*

The finished size of the Swirling Fans quilt is 44″ (112 cm) × 66″ (167.5 cm).

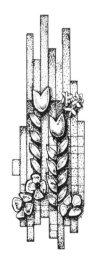

Materials

One Baltimore Medley from American Beauty Fabrics (see Sources) in ¼ yard (.23 m) pieces or ¼ yard (.23 m) each of ten fabrics for fan blades

3 yards (2.76 m) quilt top/background and binding fabric (I used black)

2½ yards (2.30 m) fan lining fabric (can be same as background fabric)

4 yards (3.68 m) backing fabric cut into two 2-yard (1.84 m) lengths and pieced together

Matching thread

Batting

Instructions

Note: All seam allowances are ¼″ (6 mm) unless specified otherwise. Patterns appear at the end of the chapter.

1. Prepare the fabrics and patterns as instructed in "Fabric Preparation" and "How to Transfer Patterns" in The Basics.

2. Cut twenty-four 11½″ (29.3 cm) squares from the background fabric. Using the fan placement–topstitching template, transfer the fan placement markings to the right sides of twenty of the background pieces.

3. Using the fan blade pattern, cut ten fan pieces from one of the fan blade fabrics. Lay the fan blade pieces in a pile. Cut ten blades from a second fabric, and lay these pieces in a pile. Continue in this manner until you have a pile for each of the ten fabrics. Arrange the ten piles in the order in which you'd like the fabrics to appear in the quilt. The first five piles of fabric will be considered set #1 of fabrics and the second five piles will be considered set #2 (Fig. 7-2).

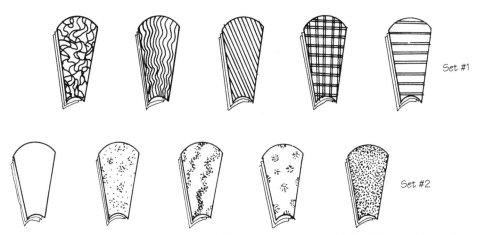

Fig. 7-2 *Arrange the piles of fan blade pieces into two sets of five fabrics each, in the order in which they will appear in the quilt.*

4. From set #1, take one blade from each pile. Stitch the long edges of the five fan blade pieces together to form one fan (Fig. 7-3). Press the seams open. Make nine more exactly like this first fan. Make ten fans from the second set of five fabrics.

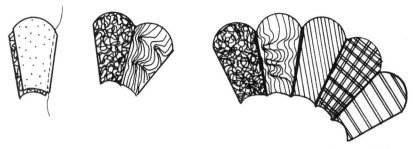

Fig. 7-3 *Take one fan blade from each pile in set #1 and stitch the five blades together along their long edges to form a fan.*

5. Lay a pieced fan, right side down, on top of the fan lining fabric, which is right side up. Pin. Cut the lining fabric to roughly match the fan. Stitch along the two curved edges, leaving the two straight side edges open (Fig. 7-4). Trim seam allowances to ⅛″ (3 mm). Turn right side out. Press. Repeat for each of the remaining 19 fans.

Fig. 7-4 *Lay a pieced fan on top of the fan lining fabric, right sides facing. Pin. Cut the lining fabric to roughly match the fan. Stitch along the curved edges, leaving the straight side edges open. Trim the seam allowances to ⅛″ (3 mm).*

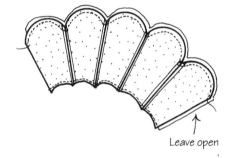

Leave open

Jumping In

I approach designing quilts in much the same way I do writing. Facing a blank screen, I start somewhere. It may be the beginning or the end. Sometimes a particular fabric inspires a vision, sometimes an idea to manipulate a pattern. Even a coupling of colors can get me started. Often I find myself amidst a pile of quilting magazines and books. Sticky notes mark pages, some of which will be fodder for the quilt developing in my mind. Clippings from magazines and catalogs, perhaps a line drawing or a color photograph, a bit of a border design—all are collected in hopes that they may fan some little spark in my imagination.

6. Lay a fan, lining side down, on the right side of a background square, matching the seams joining the fan blades to the lines marked on the background square and making sure that the top and bottom edges of the fan are even with the ends of the lines. Topstitch in the ditch along the fan seam lines. Each fan piece will arch because it is bigger than the space between the topstitching lines. Match and baste the raw side edges of the fans to the raw edges of the background squares (Fig. 7-5).

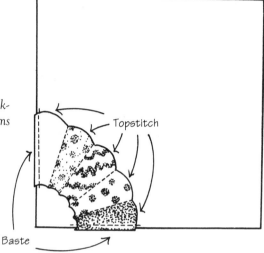

Fig. 7-5 *Lay the fans, lining side down, on the right side of the background squares, matching the seams in the fans to the placement lines marked on the squares. Topstitch along the fan seam lines.*

Topstitch

Baste

7. Following the quilt top diagram in Figure 7-1, stitch the blocks together in horizontal rows. (Don't forget to add the plain corner blocks.) Press the seams in each row in one direction. After all of the rows are constructed, stitch the rows together to form the quilt top (Fig. 7-6).

8. Lay a ruler across each of the corner squares diagonally, corner to corner. Mark. Cut along the marked lines (Fig. 7-7).

9. Put the quilt "sandwich" (quilt top, batting, backing) together and quilt. This quilt is quilted with three rows of stitching that echo the inside and outside edges of the fans. Two feathery flowers are quilted in the middle of the quilt and at the corners. Bind the quilt with the extra background fabric.

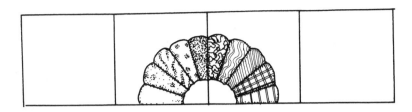

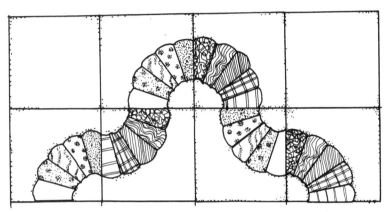

Fig. 7-6 *Lay the blocks out according to the quilt diagram in Figure 7-1. Stitch the blocks into rows. Press the seam allowances in one direction. Stitch the rows together to form the quilt top. It will be a rectangle.*

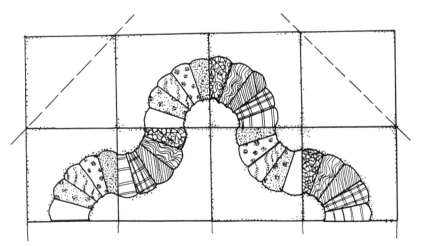

Fig. 7-7 *Mark a line from corner to corner on each corner square. Trim away the outside triangles.*

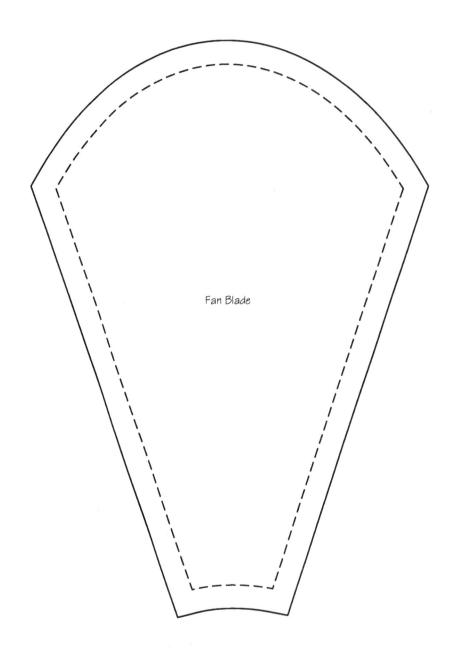

Fan Blade

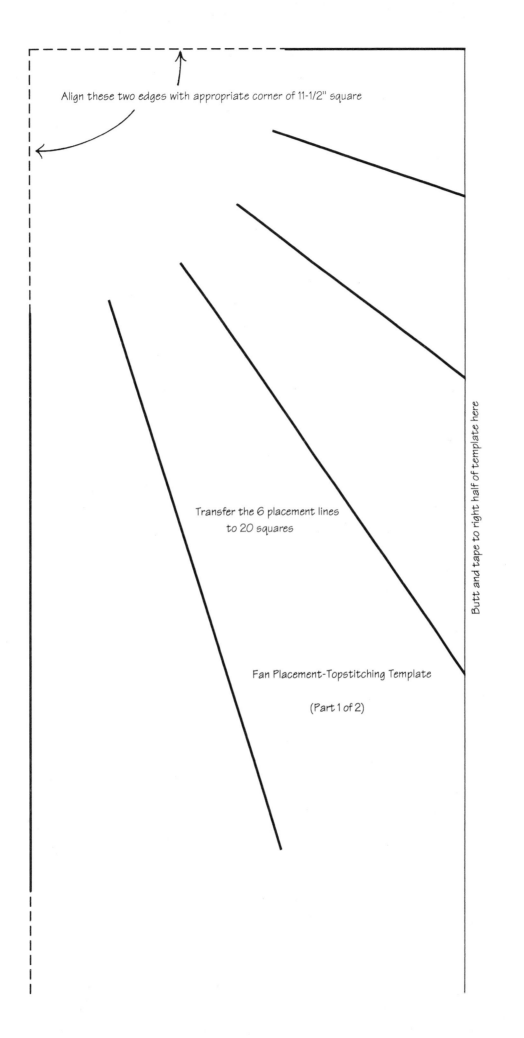

Align these two edges with appropriate corner of 11-1/2" square

Transfer the 6 placement lines
to 20 squares

Fan Placement-Topstitching Template

(Part 1 of 2)

Butt and tape to right half of template here

Fan Placement-Topstitching Template

(Part 2 of 2)

Butt and tape to left side of template here

8

Flower Basket

Any number of quilt designs that use triangles can be transformed into three-dimensional piecing. This design, based on the Bear's Paw pattern, is an example.

Rather than piece the triangles into squares, two edges are stitched, the triangle is turned right side out, and the unstitched edge is inserted into a seam. No tricky piecing!

This technique is easily adapted to many patterns. Give Lady of the Lake, Pine Tree, Bear's Paw, and Cut Glass Dish patterns three dimensions with this free-flying triangle technique. Now you can add new dimension to your favorite pattern!

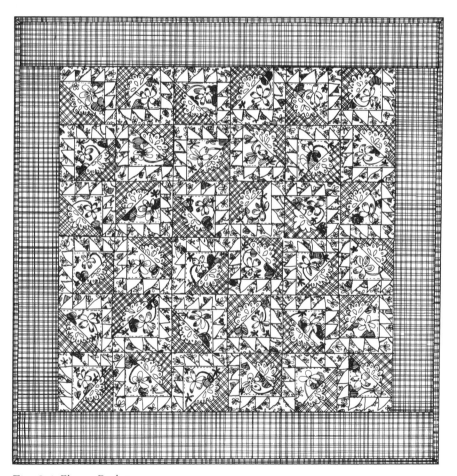

Fig. 8-1 *Flower Basket*

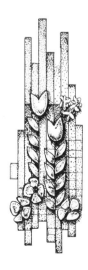

The finished size of the Flower Basket quilt is 55″ (139.5 cm) square.

Materials

1¾ yard (1.61 m) fabric for the three-dimensional triangles (green check)

1⅝ yards (1.49 m) background fabric (small pansy print)

1⅝ yards (1.49 m) basket and border fabric (multicolored check)

Eighteen 4″ (10 cm) doilies (see Home Sew in Sources)

Matching thread

Batting

½ yard (.46 m) binding fabric

Fray-stopping liquid, such as Fray Check

Instructions

Note: All seam allowances are ¼″ (6 mm) unless specified otherwise. Patterns appear at the end of the chapter.

1. Prepare the fabrics and patterns as instructed in "Fabric Preparation" and "How to Transfer Patterns" in The Basics.

2. Using the large triangle pattern, cut 36 flower triangles from the background fabric.

3. Using background strip patterns I and II, cut 36 of each from the remaining background fabric.

4. From the border fabric, cut two border strips 5″ (12.5 cm) × 45½″ (116 cm) and two border strips 5″ (12.5 cm) × 54½″ (138.5 cm). From the remaining border fabric, cut 36 basket triangles, using the large triangle pattern.

5. Fold the fabric for the three-dimensional triangles (green check) in half, right sides facing. Trace the three-dimensional triangle pattern onto the fabric. Repeat until you have 216 of them traced. Do not cut out the triangles yet.

6. Stitch along two sides of each traced triangle as shown in Figure 8-2, leaving one perpendicular edge unstitched. Cut out each triangle by trimming to ⅛″ (3 mm) outside of the stitching on the two stitched sides and cutting along the traced unstitched edge (Fig. 8-3). Turn each triangle right side out. Press.

7. Fold the doilies in half and cut along the crease. Apply Fray Check to the cut edges. Set aside to dry.

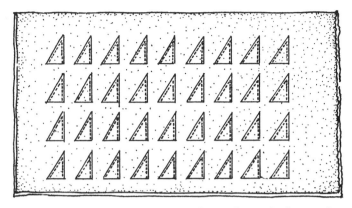

Fig. 8-2 *Stitch along two sides of each traced triangle, leaving the other edge unstitched.*

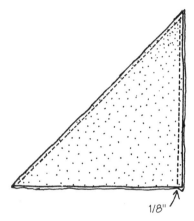

Fig. 8-3 *Trim the seam allowances of each triangle to* ¹/₈″ *(3 mm) along the stitched edges. On the unstitched edge, cut along the marked solid line.*

1/8"

8. Lay one-half of a doily right side up on a border-fabric basket triangle that is also right side up. Match centers (Fig. 8-4a). Lay one background-fabric flower triangle on top of the doily and border-fabric triangle, right side down, matching raw edges. Stitch (Fig. 8-4b). Press seam allowances to one side, and press the block open. Repeat for the remaining 35 blocks.

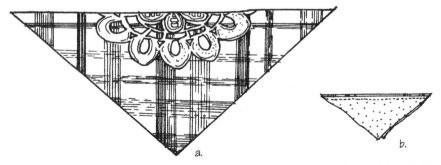

a.

b.

Fig. 8-4 *Lay a doily-half right side up on top of the right side of a border-fabric basket triangle, along the triangle's long diagonal edge. Place a background-fabric flower triangle right side down on top of them. Stitch along the long edge.*

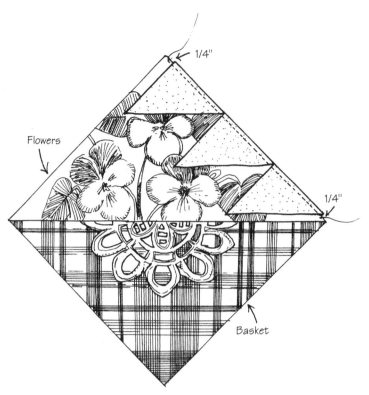

Fig. 8-5 *Matching raw edges, pin a small 3-D triangle ¼″ (6 mm) from each end of one edge of a background triangle. Place a third triangle in between these two. Pin and baste.*

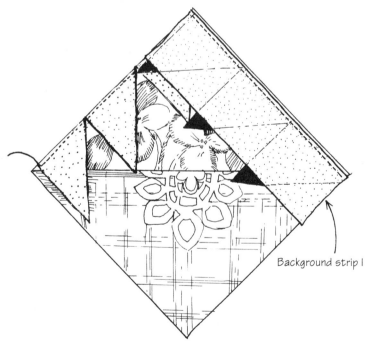

Fig. 8-6 *Matching raw edges, place one background strip I right side down on top of the right-hand edge of the flowered triangle. Stitch.*

9. Align the raw edges of three of the three-dimensional triangles along one raw edge of a background-fabric flower triangle, right sides facing, as shown in Figure 8-5. Place each of the two end triangles ¼″ (6 mm) from the appropriate raw edge, and space the center triangle evenly between them. Pin and baste. Repeat for the other edge of the background triangle.

10. Turn the block so that it forms a diamond, with the background triangle at the top. This diamond is the "basket of flowers." Lay one background strip I piece, right side down, on top of the right-hand edge of the background triangle so that it covers the small triangles on that edge. Match raw edges and stitch (Fig. 8-6). Press the strip and triangles open, pressing the seam allowances toward the large background triangle.

11. Lay one background strip II piece, right side down, on top of the other small-triangle side of the square, matching the strip's raw edges with the other strip and the background triangle. Stitch. Press open both strips and their attached small triangles (Fig. 8-7), pressing the seam allowances toward the large background triangle. Add small triangles and background strips to the remaining 35 blocks in the same manner.

Fig. 8-7 *Stitch one background strip II to the left-hand edge of the square. Press.*

12. Lay out the blocks as they will appear in the quilt top, following the color photo of the quilt. Stitch the blocks into vertical rows. Press the seam allowances in one direction. Stitch the rows together to form a square. Press the seam allowances in one direction.

13. With raw edges even and right sides facing, stitch each of the short border strips to opposite edges of the quilt top (Fig. 8-8). Press the seam allowances toward the border pieces.

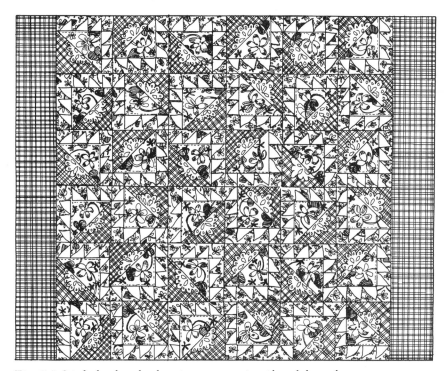

Fig. 8-8 *Stitch the short border pieces to opposite sides of the quilt top.*

Remaining Flexible

The creative process doesn't have a definite beginning and ending. When I set out to design a doll or a quilt, my first idea may transform itself into two dolls or two quilts. One of the ideas I have for a piece may not work with the rest of the design, and so it requires a separate project.

Or I may start a quilt and find I'm not ready to go on to the next step. The Quilt Muse hasn't shown me the way. I can't see the completed design or project yet, so I set it aside. Being patient and trusting that new ideas will come are important habits for the quilt designer to cultivate.

14. With raw edges even and right sides facing, stitch each of the long border pieces to the two remaining edges of the quilt top (Fig. 8-9). Press the seam allowances toward the border.

15. Put the quilt "sandwich" (quilt top, batting, backing) together and quilt. Quilt in the ditch around the basket/background squares and above the tops of the baskets. I quilted the border along the stripes. Bind the quilt.

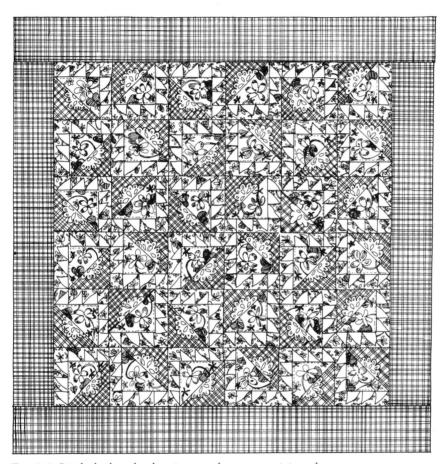

Fig. 8-9 *Stitch the long border pieces to the two remaining edges.*

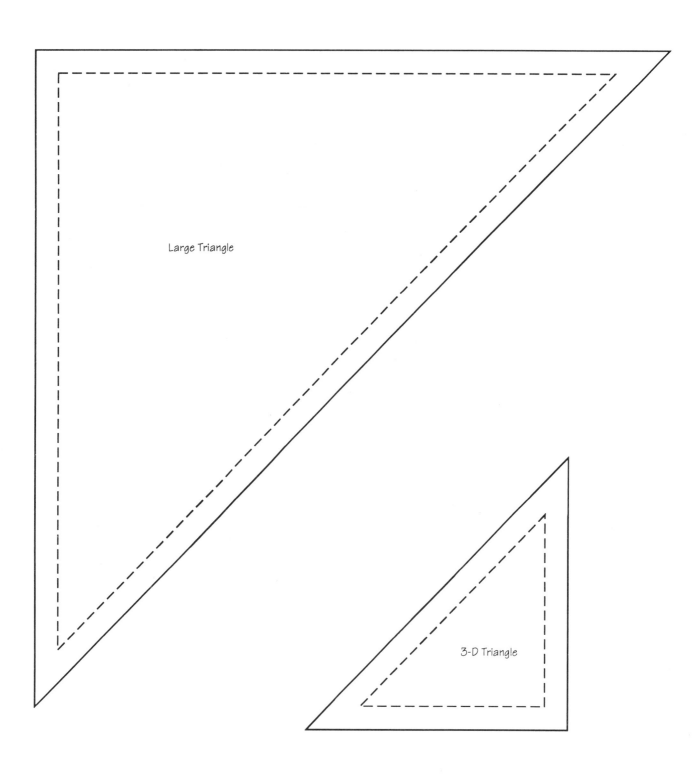

Large Triangle

3-D Triangle

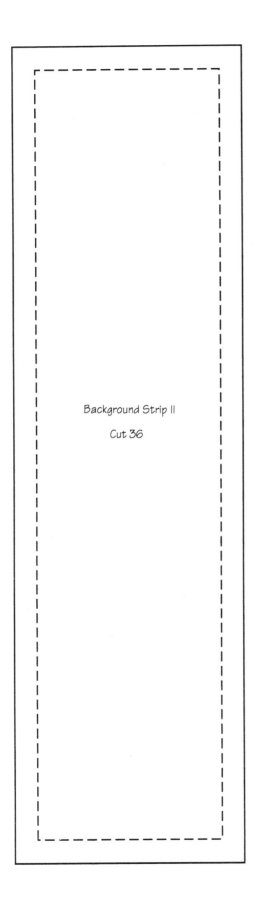

Background Strip II

Cut 36

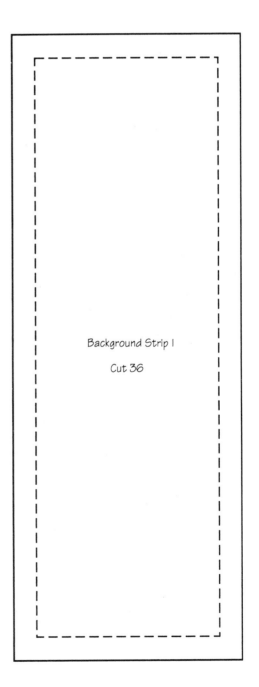

Background Strip I

Cut 36

New Ideas in Three Dimensions

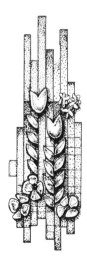

Twisted Ribbons

9

Sometimes a quilt turns out quite unlike my original vision. The Twisted Ribbons quilt turned out much better.

I set out to twist double-sided bias fabric from corner to corner of the blocks of the quilt top, two bias strips for each block, crossing in an "X." What could be simpler? So, I cut all of them out. You know what's coming.

The twisting didn't work the way I had expected and I had to re-think my design. I fooled around with the strips by twisting and otherwise manipulating them. For some reason, I folded a pair of strips. That was it! In no time I had the beginnings of the quilt on the design wall (see the boxed note on page 31).

Folded, double-sided "ribbons" are inserted into the seams between the blocks. The arrangement of the blocks forms swirling pinwheels.

Each of the two ribbons is two fabric strips sewn together along their long edges. When the ribbon is folded, the second fabric is visible. Two different fabrics are paired to form two different ribbons; one of each is used on each block. I used bright designer cottons for my quilt. As an alternative, imagine the shimmer of silk catching the light or the subtle effect of hand-dyed fabrics.

It seems so easy in retrospect.

The finished size of the Twisted Ribbons quilt is 36″ (91.5 cm) square.

Materials

1⅜ yards (1.27 m) background and border fabric

1 yard (.92 m) each of four "ribbon" fabrics (I paired two orange/reds and two purples)

1¼ yards (1.38 m) fabric for backing and binding

Matching thread

Batting

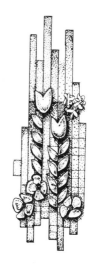

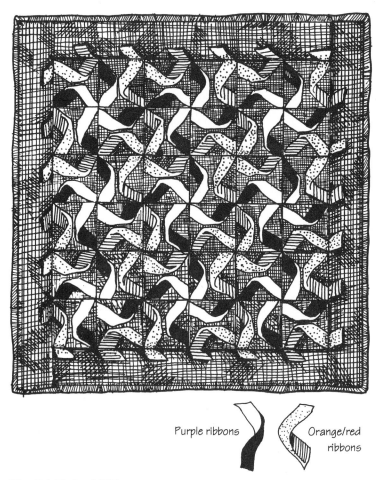

Purple ribbons   Orange/red ribbons

Fig. 9-1 *Twisted Ribbons*

Instructions

Note: All seam allowances are ¼" (6 mm) unless specified otherwise. Patterns appear at the end of the chapter.

1. Prepare the fabrics and patterns as instructed in "Fabric Preparation" and "How to Transfer Patterns" in The Basics.

2. Cut the background fabric into thirty-six 5" (12.5 cm) squares. For the border, cut two 27½" (70 cm) × 5" (12.5 cm) pieces and two 36½" (93 cm) × 5" (12.5 cm) pieces from the same fabric.

3. Cut each of the ribbon fabrics into 2½" (6.5 cm) wide bias strips.

4. With right sides facing, match the long raw edges of one pair of ribbon strips (either two orange/reds or two purples). Stitch one edge. Press the seam allowances open. Stitch the remaining long raw edges together. Press seam open (Fig. 9-2). Repeat for all the orange/red strips and then for all the purple strips. Turn all of the stitched ribbon strips right side out. Press them flat.

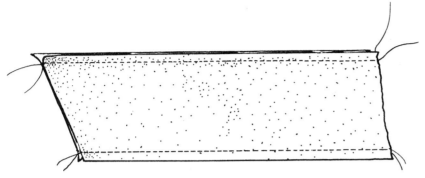

Fig. 9-2 *Stitched ribbon strip.*

5. Using the ribbon pattern, cut 36 ribbons from the stitched strips of each fabric combination—36 orange/red and 36 of the two purples (Fig. 9-3a). Using the ribbon end pattern, cut 24 ribbon ends from the stitched strips of one of the fabric combinations (Fig. 9-3b). I used orange/red.

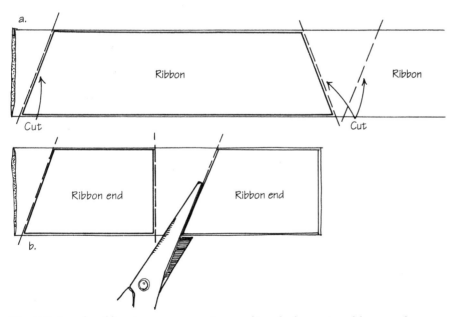

Fig. 9-3 *Lay the ribbon pattern on a strip, matching the long top and bottom edges. Cut along the short, angled ends. Cut the ribbon ends in the same way.*

6. Starting with one color set (such as orange/red), baste one end of a ribbon piece to the corner of one background square, raw edges even, as shown in Figure 9-4.

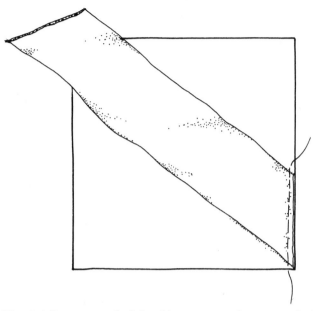

Fig. 9-4 *Baste one end of the ribbon pieces to the corner of a background square.*

7. Fold the ribbon piece and stitch the other end to the adjacent edge of the background square (Fig. 9-5). Repeat for the remaining background squares.

8. Baste one of the other ribbon pieces (in this case, the two purples) to the background squares on the remaining two raw edges (Fig. 9-6).

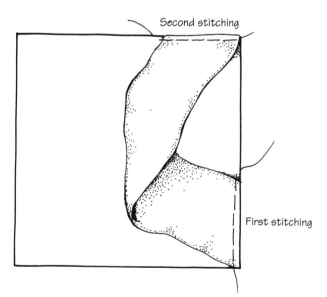

Second stitching

First stitching

Fig. 9-5 *Fold the ribbon piece so that the other fabric shows. Baste the loose end to the adjacent edge of the background square.*

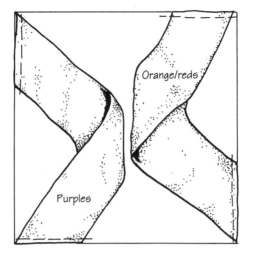

Fig. 9-6 *Baste the ends of the second ribbon piece to the background square.*

9. Following the quilt diagram in Figure 9-1, lay out the ribbon blocks into a large square of six blocks by six blocks, turning the blocks to match the diagram.

10. Starting at one corner, stitch the blocks together to form rows, catching the basting *inside* the stitching (Fig. 9-7). On the back of each strip, press the seam allowances of the first row up. Press those of the second row down, and so forth. Stitch the rows together, matching seams. Press the seam allowances to one side.

Fig. 9-7 *Stitch the ribbon blocks into rows.*

11. Baste the ribbon end pieces to the ends of the orange/red ribbon pieces, right sides together, all around the edge of the quilt (Figs. 9-8a and b). I matched right sides of the same color together.

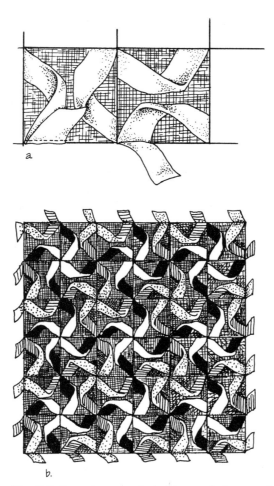

Fig. 9-8 *Baste the orange/red ribbon end pieces to the ends of the orange/red ribbons all the way around the edge of the quilt, matching orange to orange and red to red.*

12. Keeping the ribbon ends flat against the quilt top, pin the short (27½" [70 cm]) border strips along opposite edges of the quilt top, right sides facing and raw edges even. Stitch. Press the seam allowances toward the border. Open up the border strips (Fig. 9-9).

13. With the ribbon ends flat against the quilt top, pin the long (36½" [93 cm]) border strips to the remaining two edges of the quilt top, right sides facing and raw edges even. Stitch, catching the basting on the ribbons inside the stitching. Press the seam allowances toward the border. Open up the border strips (Fig. 9-10).

14. Layer the quilt top, batting, and backing. Quilt. This quilt is stitched in the ditch between the blocks. A design mimicking the twisted ribbons is quilted along the border. Bind.

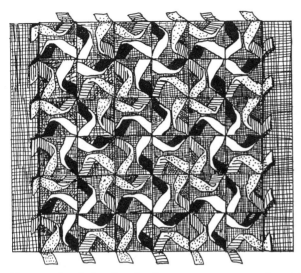

Fig. 9-9 *Stitch the short border strips to opposite sides of the quilt top.*

Fig. 9-10 *Stitch the long border strips to the remaining edges of the quilt top.*

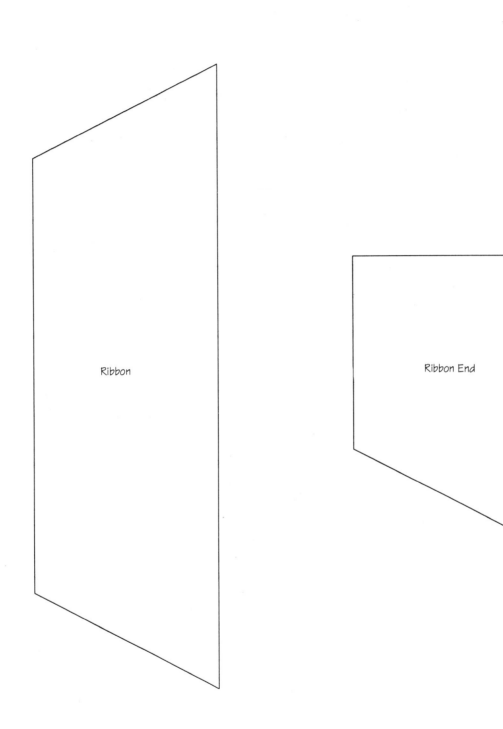

Ribbon

Ribbon End

Interlocking Squares Two Ways

10

Make a bold geometric statement with this easy quilt. The Interlocking Squares pattern is made by inserting colored fabric into the seams of the background squares and rectangles as they are pieced.

Instructions are given for two variations. For the first, the colored fabrics that form the Interlocking Squares are frayed. To achieve this, the folded fabric strips are clipped after construction. When the quilt is laundered, the raw edges of the colorful Interlocking Squares fray. For the second version, the colored strips are gathered before piecing them into the seams. The finished edges of the colored strips form wavy squares that stand straight up from the quilt top.

Once in awhile a quilt design appears magically and, when sewn, turns out exactly as envisioned. Such was the case with Interlocking Squares. I was struggling with the three-dimensional Double Wedding Ring quilt at the time. I wanted to fold long strips of fabric that were cut on the bias around strips of batting and insert their seam allowances into the curved seams of the pieced quilt top to form the Double Wedding Ring pattern. Bunching at the intersections where the "rings" butted nixed the idea. The vision of the interlocking rings suddenly turned into squares. Eureka! The computer made quick work of the simple design, and there I was staring at my Interlocking Squares quilt in color on the screen. Making it in fabric was just as easy.

I remembered all the fun I had with the Frayed Log Cabin quilt made for my previous book, *Three-Dimensional Appliqué*, and so decided on the frayed effect for this design, too. After making the quilt, I laundered it and voilà—it worked!

For those who blanch at the thought of breaking the hide-those-seam-allowances rule, I have included an alternative version of the quilt. (Yes, I listened when friends reported comments about the exposed seam allowances on my Frayed Log Cabin quilt.) I can see how this may seem akin to wearing one's clothes inside out. So for a finished option, I made the quilt with gathered, rather than frayed, inserts. I hope you're as pleased with the results as I was.

The finished size of the Interlocking Squares quilt is 33″ (84 cm) square. The frayed version may shrink a bit when washed and dried.

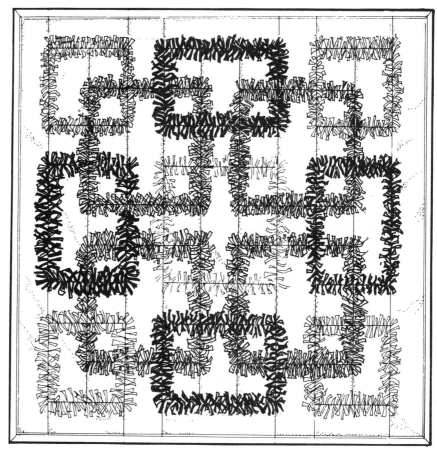

Fig. 10-1 *Interlocking Squares*

Materials

For the frayed version:

¼ yard (.23 m) red fabric
⅓ yard (.30 m) blue fabric
⅓ yard (.30 m) yellow fabric
⅛ yard (.12 m) green fabric

For the gathered version:

⅓ yard (.30 m) purple fabric
½ yard (.46 m) green fabric
⅝ yard (.57 m) pink fabric
¾ yard (.69 m) blue fabric

For both versions:

1½ yards (1.38 m) background fabric (black for frayed, gray print for gathered)

1 yard (.92 m) backing fabric

Matching thread

Batting

⅜ yard (.35 m) binding fabric

Instructions

Note: All seam allowances are ¼″ (6 mm) unless specified otherwise.

1. Prepare the fabrics as instructed in "Fabric Preparation" in The Basics.

2. For either quilt, cut the background fabric into squares and rectangles according to the following chart:

Background Fabric Cutting Chart

Size	Number to Cut
3½″ (9 cm) × 6½″ (16.5 cm)	14
3½″ (9 cm) × 3½″ (9 cm)	44
3½″ (9 cm) × 9½″ (24.5 cm)	9
3½″ (9 cm) × 33½″ (85.5 cm)	2

3. For both versions, cut the colored fabric into 2½″- (6.5 cm) wide strips along the straight of the grain of the fabric.

4. *For the frayed version:* Cut the colored strips into segments as you piece the quilt (covered in Steps 7 through 12). You'll need to make each segment the length of the background square or rectangle to which it is being attached *minus* the ¼″ (6 mm) seam allowances needed for each edge of the background piece. For example, if you are attaching a colored segment to a 3½″ (9 cm) square, cut a 3″ (7.5 cm) segment from the appropriate colored strip (3½″ [9 cm] minus the two ¼″ [6 mm] seam allowances). Fold the segment in half lengthwise, wrong sides together.

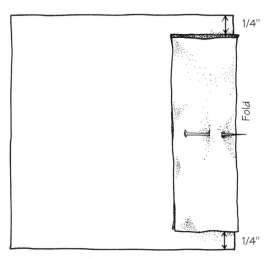

Fig. 10-2 *For the frayed version, match the folded edge of the strip to the raw edge of the square.*

Butt the folded edge of the colored segment along one raw edge of the background piece, centering the segment along the edge (Fig. 10-2).

5. *For the gathered version:* Cut the colored strips into the following number of pieces of the specified lengths:

Gathered Strips Cutting Chart

	Pieces to Cut		
Fabric	*8″ (20.5 cm)*	*16″ (40.5 cm)*	*26″ (91.5 cm)*
Purple	12		
Green	16	8	
Pink	28		4
Blue	48		

Once the strips are cut, fold each one in half lengthwise, matching the raw edges, right sides facing. Stitch along the strip's short edges (Fig. 10-3a). Trim the seam allowances. Turn the strip right side out. Press. Making sure the long raw edges match, gather stitch just under ¼″ (6 mm) from those raw edges (Fig. 10-3b).

6. *For the gathered version:* The colored strips correspond to the background pieces as follows: The 8″ (20.5 cm) strips are attached to the 3½″ (9 cm) edges of background pieces; the 16″ (40.5 cm) strips are attached to 6½″ (16.5 cm) edges; and the 26″ (91.5 cm) strips are attached to 9½″ (24.5 cm) edges. As you assemble the quilt top in Steps 7 through 12, gather the appropriate colored strip to fit within the length of the corresponding edge, leaving ¼″ (6 mm) for seam allowances on either

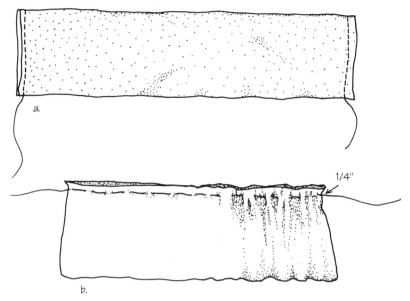

Fig. 10-3 *For the gathered version, fold the strip in half lengthwise, right sides facing. Stitch each short edge. Turn right side out and then gather a scant ¼″ (6 mm) from the raw edges.*

side of the gathered strip. For example, if a gathered strip is to be sewn to a 3½″ (9 cm) square, pin one end of the strip ¼″ (6 mm) from one raw edge of the square. Pin the other end of the strip ¼″ (6 mm) from the other raw edge. Pull up on the gather threads and adjust the strip to fit. Pin. Stitch (Fig. 10-4).

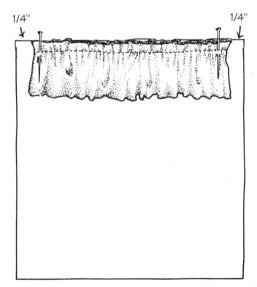

Fig. 10-4 *For the gathered version, pull up on the gather threads and adjust the gathers evenly to fit along the edge of the square or rectangle, leaving a good ¼″ (6 mm) of square or rectangle at each end of the strip.*

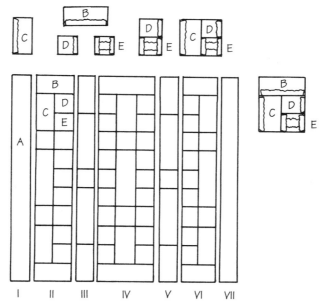

Fig. 10-5 *Create sections I through VII of the quilt top by stitching colored strips to background pieces as indicated.*

7. The quilt is constructed in vertical sections (marked I through VII in Fig. 10-5). Use Figures 10-1 and 10-5, as well as the color photos of the quilts, to guide you through the piecing. Steps 8 through 11 will help you get started by showing you how to piece the top of section II. From there, you will be able to construct the rest of the quilt by following Step 12 and the illustrations and photos.

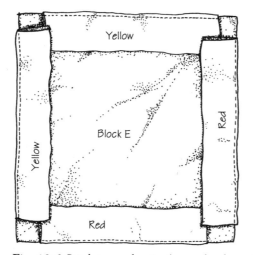

Fig. 10-6 *Stitch two red strips (green for the gathered quilt) to two adjacent edges of a background square. Stitch two yellow strips (blue for the gathered version) to the two remaining edges. Frayed version shown.*

8. Start at the top of section II with a 3½″ (9 cm) background square. Stitch an 8″ (20.5 cm) green strip for the gathered quilt, or a 3″ (7.5 cm) red strip for the frayed version, to one raw edge of the background square. Stitch another strip of the same color and size (green for gathered; red for frayed) to an adjacent edge of the square. In the same manner, stitch two 8″ (20.5 cm) blue strips for the gathered quilt, or two 3″ (7.5 cm) yellow strips for the frayed quilt, to the two remaining edges of the background square to create block E. (Frayed version is shown in Fig. 10-6.)

9. To create block D, stitch an 8″ (20.5 cm) green strip for the gathered quilt, or a 3″ (7.5 cm) red strip for the frayed version, to one raw edge of a 3½″ (9 cm) background square. For block C, stitch a 16″ (40.5 cm) green strip for the gathered version, or a 6″ (15 cm) red strip for the frayed quilt, to one long edge of a 3½″ (9 cm) × 6½″ (16.5 cm) background rectangle. For block B, make a duplicate of block C.

10. Stitch blocks D and E together. (Frayed version is shown in Fig. 10-7.) Be careful not to catch the free ends of the strips in the seams as you stitch.

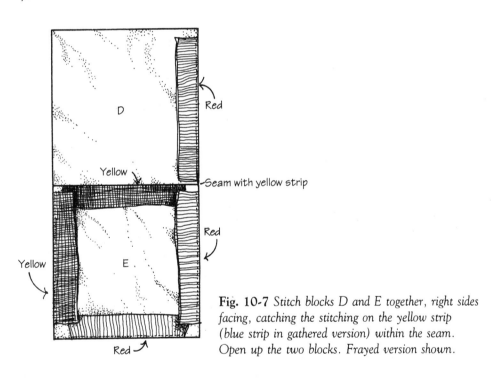

Fig. 10-7 *Stitch blocks D and E together, right sides facing, catching the stitching on the yellow strip (blue strip in gathered version) within the seam. Open up the two blocks. Frayed version shown.*

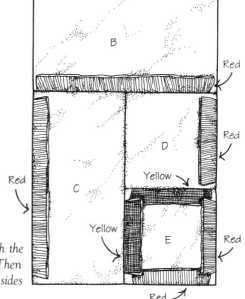

Fig. 10-8 *With right sides facing, stitch the combined block D and E to block C. Then stitch the whole thing to block B, right sides facing. Frayed version shown.*

11. Stitch block C to the combined D and E block. Then stitch block B to the combined C, D, and E block. (Frayed version is shown in Fig. 10-8.)

12. Use Figures 10-1 and 10-5 and the color photos of the quilts to continue piecing the quilt top, forming sections I through VII. Add the colored strips as you go, making sure you're using the proper size strip (see Steps 4 and 5) and the proper color of strip (refer to the color photos). You may attach the colored strips to the background piece on either side of it, because the strip will stand up from the finished quilt top.

13. Layer the quilt top, batting, and backing. Quilt. I quilted ½″ (1.3 cm) away from the seam inserts. Bind the quilt.

14. *For the frayed quilt:* Cut into the colored strips, starting at their raw edges and ending almost at the background fabric, making the cuts about every ¼″ (6 mm). To fray the colored strips, machine wash and dry the quilt.

Eagle's View

11

Soaring above a crazy-patched landscape of hills and blue sky, this three-dimensional eagle is stitched separately from the quilt top. Only the tops of the eagle's wings are attached, by insertion into the seam between the sky and hills.

Likewise, the sun's rays are stitched into the seams joining the sun to the sky.

Eagle's View begs the question, When is it appliqué and when is it piecing?

This quilt was a commission for an award. The request was for a quilt of about 3-foot square depicting an eagle. Because I was working on this book at the time, I challenged myself to find a way to create an eagle pieced in three dimensions.

The spark took awhile in coming, but one night I sat down with the germ of this idea and sketched it out.

Yes, the eagle could easily be appliquéd to the quilt. Inserting the wings into the seams, though, gives the bird a free-flying look, unattainable with appliqué.

Fig. 11-1 *Eagle's View*

The Eagle's View quilt measures 31″ (78.5 cm) × 36″ (91.5 cm).

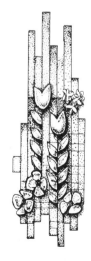

Materials

Large scraps of yellow fabrics for sun, rays, and beak
Large scraps of blue fabrics for sky
Large scraps of green fabrics for hills
Scraps of white fabrics for eagle's head and tail
Scraps of black fabrics for eagle's body and wings
Large scrap of fusible interfacing
Matching thread
Polyester fiberfill stuffing
Black marker, such as a Micron Pigma
Yellow paint or marker
Batting
Drawing paper
1¼ yards (1.15 m) fabric for backing and binding

Instructions

Note: *All seam allowances are ¼″ (6 mm) unless specified otherwise. Patterns appear at the end of the chapter.*

1. Prepare the fabrics and patterns as instructed in "Fabric Preparation" and "How to Transfer Patterns" in The Basics.

2. Tape together large pieces of drawing paper until you have a piece measuring 31″ (78.5 cm) × 36″ (91.5 cm) or larger. If larger, draw a rectangle 31″ (78.5 cm) × 36″ (91.5 cm). Draw lines on the paper to

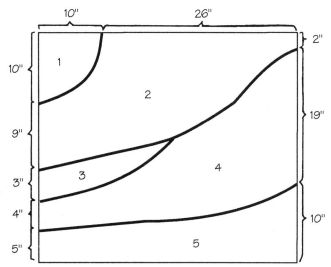

Fig. 11-2 *Divide your large piece of paper into five sections, using the heavy lines and measurements on the diagram as guidelines.*

designate the hills, horizon, and sun, much like the heavy lines in Figure 11-2. Mark the sections 1, 2, 3, 4, and 5. This will help you put them back together properly and also designate the right side and top and bottom of the pieces. Cut the pieces out along the heavy lines.

3. Piece together enough fabrics to cover each paper section of your quilt top, except the sun (Fig. 11-3). Use sky fabrics for section 2 and mountain fabrics for sections 3, 4, and 5. Don't worry about the shape of each piece; just make sure the pieced sections are larger than the paper pieces. Press all seam allowances to one side.

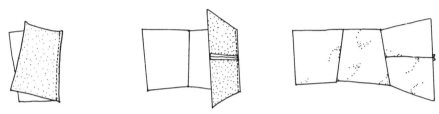

Fig. 11-3 *Piece fabrics together to create each section of the quilt top. Make each pieced section of fabric larger than the corresponding paper piece.*

4. Lay down a pieced section of fabric right side up. Lay the appropriate paper pattern on top, also right side up (Fig. 11-4). Pin. Cut the pieced fabric ¼″ (6 mm) larger than the pattern all the way around. Repeat for the remaining paper pattern sections and set them aside.

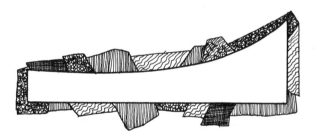

Fig. 11-4 *Lay the paper pieces on top of the pieced fabric sections, both right sides up. Cut the fabric ¼″ (6 mm) larger than the paper pattern all the way around.*

5. For the sun, choose a piece of yellow fabric twice as large as the sun paper piece. Wet the fabric. Gather the fabric up into a ball. Secure the ball with rubber bands or strings and toss it in the dryer. Take the ball out of the dryer when it is half dry and remove the rubber bands. Gently pull the fabric out, wrong side up, maintaining the wrinkles in the fabric. If you pull at it too much you will lose the wrinkles and have to start over. Fuse the interfacing to the wrong side of the fabric.

6. Lay the sun paper pattern on the right side of the wrinkled sun fabric. Pin. Cut the fabric ¼″ (6 mm) larger than the sun pattern.

7. Using the two sun ray patterns, cut five sun rays, two from one pattern and three from the other. Flip the patterns and repeat. Match each ray with its mirror image, right sides facing. Stitch the pairs together, leaving the straight edges open as shown in Figure 11-5, to create five rays. Trim seam allowances to ⅛″ (3 mm). Turn right side out. Press and set aside.

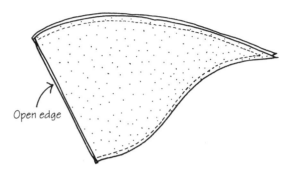

Fig. 11-5 *Stitch the sun rays, leaving the straight edges open.*

8. Cut the eagle pattern apart: beak, head, body, and tail. Take the pieced-together right and left wing patterns you created in Step 1 and make a second copy of each completed wing pattern.

9. Take one right wing pattern and one left wing pattern and cut them each into two pieces: an upper and a lower wing. Take one upper wing pattern piece and place it wrong side down on a piece of wing fabric that is right side up (wing fabric may need to be pieced first, as in Step 3). Cut the fabric ¼″ (6 mm) outside of the edges of the paper pattern.

10. A flip-and-sew piecing method is used to make the corresponding lower wing. Place one end of the lower wing pattern, right (printed) side up, on top of two scraps of right-sides-facing black fabric. Stitch along the first flip-and-sew stitching line marked on the paper pattern, sewing through the paper and both layers of fabric. Trim the fabric as indicated in Figure 11-6 to create seam allowances of about ¼″ (6 mm).

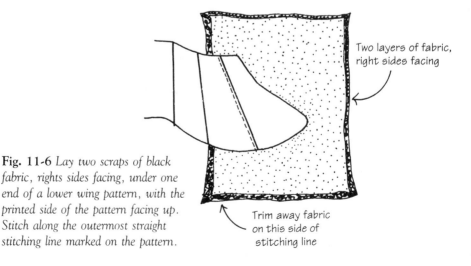

Fig. 11-6 *Lay two scraps of black fabric, rights sides facing, under one end of a lower wing pattern, with the printed side of the pattern facing up. Stitch along the outermost straight stitching line marked on the pattern.*

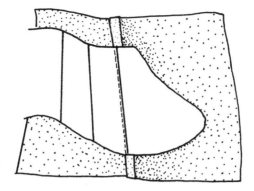

Fig. 11-7 *Fold the bottommost fabric out so that the wrong sides of both fabrics face the paper.*

11. Fold the bottom fabric out so that the wrong sides of both fabrics are against the paper (Fig. 11-7).

12. Keeping the fabric open and the pattern piece right side up, place a third piece of wing fabric underneath the first two pieces, right sides facing (Fig. 11-8). Stitch along the next marked stitching line through the three layers (paper pattern and second and third pieces of fabric). Trim the fabric seam allowances as indicated on Figure 11-8 and fold out the third piece of fabric as you did for the second piece in Step 11. Continue in this same manner until you complete the lower wing.

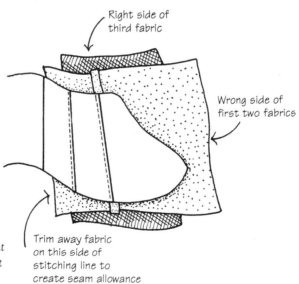

Right side of
third fabric

Wrong side of
first two fabrics

Fig. 11-8 *Add a third piece of fabric to the first two pieces, right sides facing. Stitch along the next stitching line.*

Trim away fabric
on this side of
stitching line to
create seam allowance

13. Trim the fabric ¼″ (6 mm) away from the outer edges of the lower wing pattern piece. Tear the paper away. Stitch the lower wing and upper wing together, right sides facing (Fig. 11-9). Trim the seam allowances to ⅛″ (3 mm) and press them toward the top of the wing.

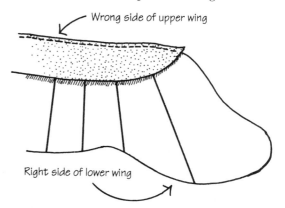

Wrong side of upper wing

Right side of lower wing

Fig. 11-9 *With right sides facing, stitch the lower and upper wings together.*

14. Lay the pieced wing, right side down, on the right side of more black fabric (the underwing). Lay both pieces on top of a piece of batting. Stitch, leaving the straight edges unstitched and leaving a gap in the stitching between the dots at the top of the wing as shown in Figure 11-10. Trim seam allowances where you stitched to ⅛″ (3 mm). Turn the wing right side out through one of the gaps. Repeat for the other wing.

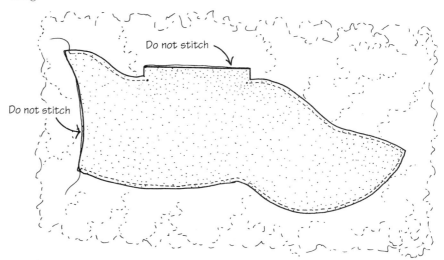

Do not stitch

Do not stitch

Fig. 11-10 *With right sides facing, place the pieced wing on top of black fabric for the underwing. Lay both pieces of fabric on top of a piece of batting. Stitch, leaving the straight edges unstitched and leaving a gap in the stitching between the dots at the top of the wing.*

15. Using the beak pattern, cut out two beaks from the yellow fabric. With right sides facing, stitch the two beak pieces together, leaving the straight edge open. Trim seam allowances to ⅛″ (3 mm). Turn right side out (Fig. 11-11).

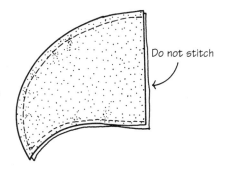

Do not stitch

Fig. 11-11 *With right sides facing, stitch two beak pieces together, leaving the straight edge unstitched. Trim the seam allowances to ⅛″ (3 mm).*

16. Using the tail pattern, cut two tails from the white fabric. Lay the fabric tails, right sides facing, on top of a piece of batting. Stitch the tails together, stitching through the fabric and the batting but leaving the concave edge of the tail unstitched. Trim seam allowances to ⅛″ (3 mm). Turn the tail right side out. Topstitch through all layers along the lines marked on the pattern (Fig. 11-12).

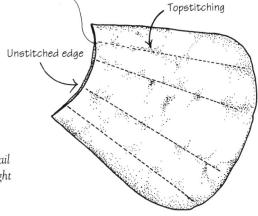

Topstitching

Unstitched edge

Fig. 11-12 *After sewing the two tail pieces together and turning them right side out, topstitch the tail along the marked lines through all layers.*

17. Using the head pattern, cut out two heads from the white fabric. Using the body pattern, cut out two bodies from the black fabric. With right sides facing, pin and stitch a head piece to a body piece, matching dots so that you pair the correct head and body (Fig. 11-13). Repeat for the other head and body.

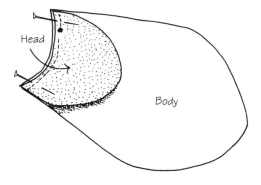

Head

Body

Fig. 11-13 *With right sides facing, pin and stitch a head piece to a body piece, matching dots so that you pair the correct head and body pieces.*

18. Pin the beak to the right side of one head between the appropriate dots. Pin the tail to the right side of the attached body. Baste (Fig. 11-14).

19. Keeping the beak and tail as shown in Figure 11-14, pin the two body/head pieces together, right sides facing. Stitch from dot to dot around the head and from dot to dot around the lower body (Fig. 11-15).

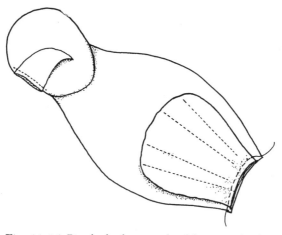

Fig. 11-14 *Pin the beak to one head between the dots. Pin the tail to the attached body. Baste.*

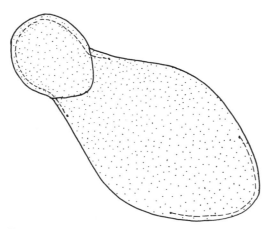

Fig. 11-15 *Stitch from dot to dot around the head and from dot to dot around the lower body.*

20. Hold the eagle's body so that the seam into which the beak is inserted faces left. Cut a slash in the top layer of fabric on the eagle's body (Fig. 11-16). This side will be against the quilt when the eagle is turned right side out.

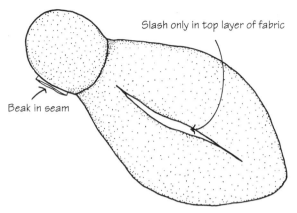

Fig. 11-16 *Cut a slash in the top layer of fabric on the eagle's body.*

21. Insert the left wing, right (pieced) side down, into the slashed opening and through the right opening in the side seam of the eagle as shown in Figure 11-17. Pin. Stitch between the dots. Repeat this process for the right wing, slipping it into the slash and through the opposite opening. The two wing ends will be sticking out of the slashed opening. Turn the eagle right side out through the slash. Stuff the eagle with polyester fiberfill. Whipstitch the slash on the back of the body closed.

22. Draw the eagle's eye with the black marker. Using yellow paint or a marker, color the eagle's pupil. Then fill in the iris with black.

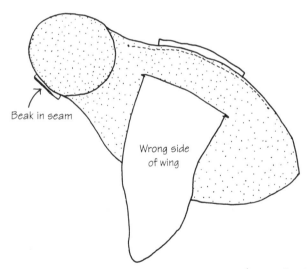

Fig. 11-17 *Insert the left wing, right side down, into the slashed opening and through the right opening in the side seam of the eagle. Pin. Stitch between the dots.*

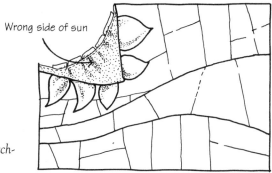

Wrong side of sun

Fig. 11-18 *Stitch the sun to the sky, including the rays in the stitching.*

23. Lay out the three hill pieces as they will appear in the finished quilt. Pin and stitch the pieces together. Pin and baste the sun's rays to the sky. Stitch the sun to the sky, including the rays in the seam (Fig. 11-18).

24. Baste the seams joining the sky and hill together. Position the eagle on the quilt top. Pin the tabs at the tops of the wings over two basted seams as shown in Figure 11-19. Remove the basting stitches of these seams and insert the wing tabs. Restitch, including the wing tabs in the seams.

Fig. 11-19 *Decide where you want to put the eagle. The wing tabs will be inserted into the long horizontal seams between sections. Remove the basting from where you want to insert the wing tabs. Insert the wing tabs into the seams. Restitch all basted seams.*

25. Layer the quilt top, batting, and backing. Quilt. I quilted gentle curves, some emanating from the sun and stopping at the horizon and some sweeping horizontally across the green hills. I also stitched along the horizon (minus the eagle). Bind.

To Plan or To Improvise?

Some people are more comfortable planning everything on paper before they cut the first piece of fabric. Others practice a more spontaneous approach. Starting with one special piece of fabric as a background or a stitched block, the designer builds the quilt in fabric as she or he designs it, continually changing the positions of blocks—adding, subtracting, perhaps going off in an unforeseen direction—until everything is just right.

I use both methods, depending upon the design I'm working with. If I was to sit down today to build an appliqué picture, I'd prepare my background fabric, put it up on my design wall, and start cutting appliqué shapes, positioning them on the background and building and rearranging my design as I went. I might stitch down some pieces before deciding on the placement or inclusion of others.

With pieced quilts I'm more apt to draw the design out first. I may make changes or redo my blocks after I experiment with fabric, but I like to have a very good idea of how the pieces are going to fit together before I start stitching.

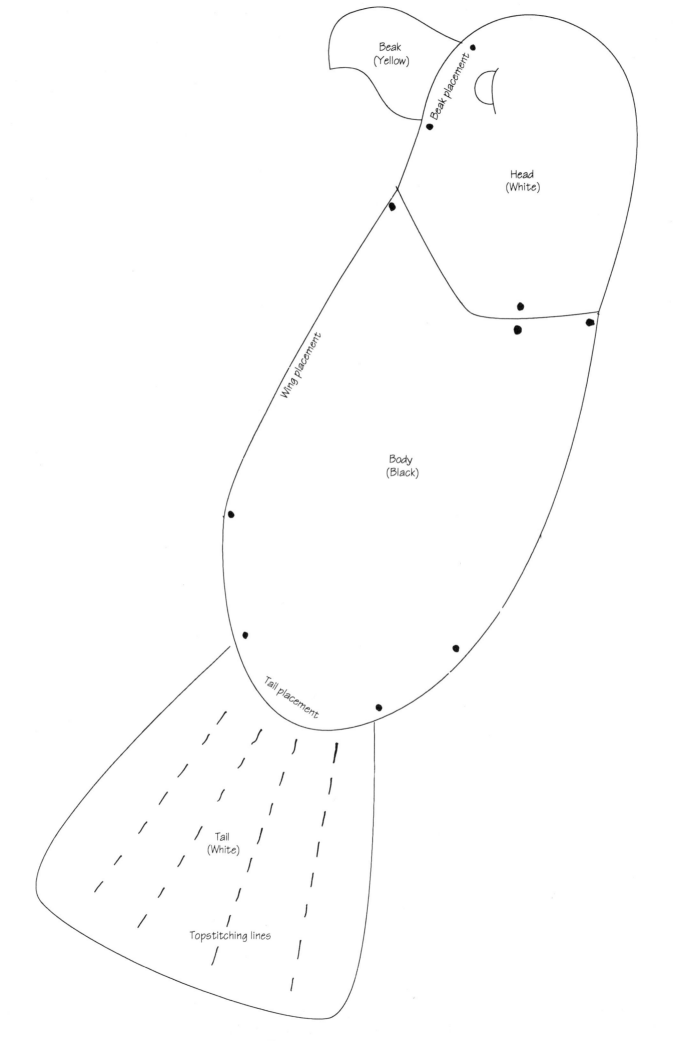

Beak
(Yellow)

Beak placement

Head
(White)

Wing placement

Body
(Black)

Tail placement

Tail
(White)

Topstitching lines

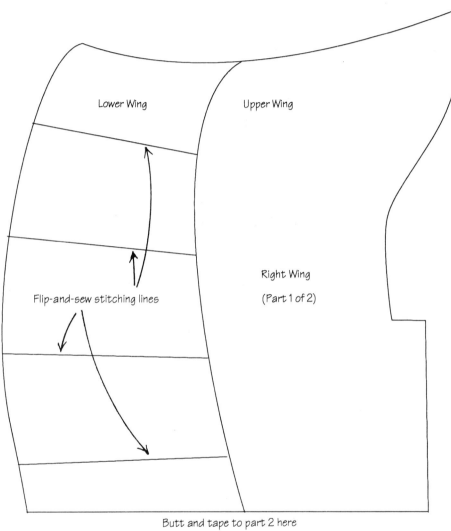

Lower Wing

Upper Wing

Flip-and-sew stitching lines

Right Wing

(Part 1 of 2)

Butt and tape to part 2 here

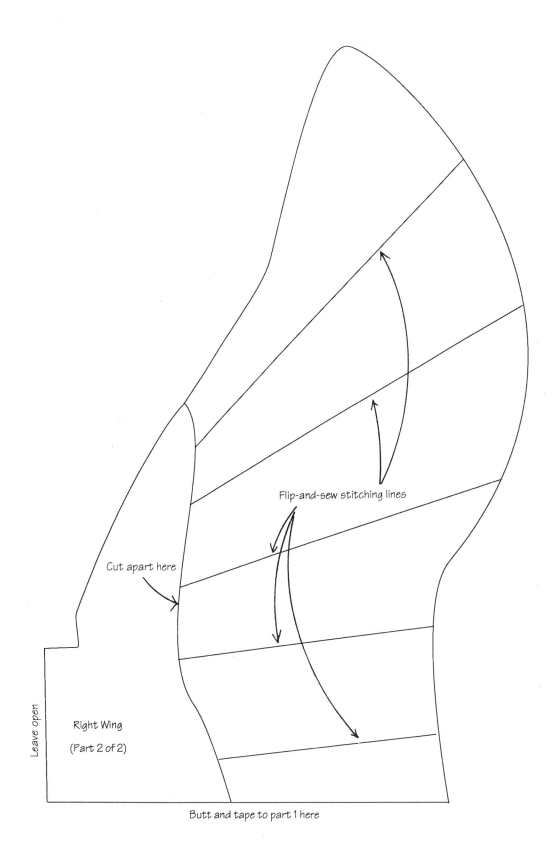

Flip-and-sew stitching lines

Cut apart here

Leave open

Right Wing

(Part 2 of 2)

Butt and tape to part 1 here

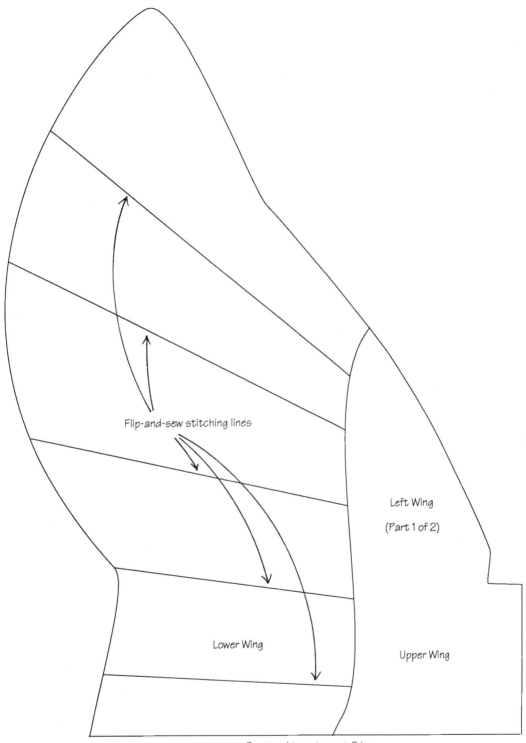

Flip-and-sew stitching lines

Left Wing

(Part 1 of 2)

Lower Wing

Upper Wing

Butt and tape to part 2 here

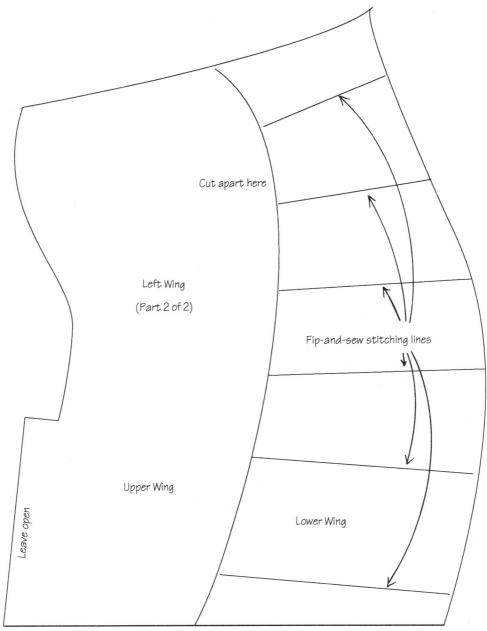

Cut apart here

Left Wing

(Part 2 of 2)

Fip-and-sew stitching lines

Upper Wing

Lower Wing

Leave open

Butt and tape to part 1 here

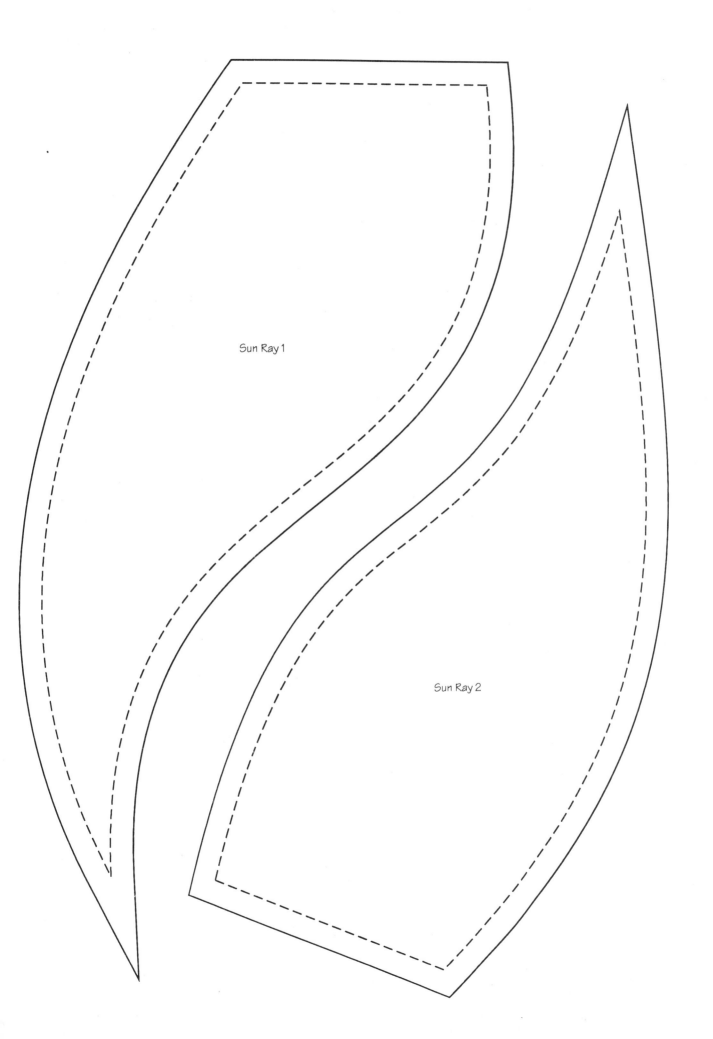

12 *Garden at Dusk*

Though this quilt looks complicated, it is actually composed of just two parts: the background, which is constructed of vertical 1″ (2.5 cm) strips, and the three-dimensional elements, which are stitched into the seams of the strips.

Due to the large number of pieces to be inserted into the seams, however, this quilt is more challenging to construct than others in the book. I've given complete instructions for making the flowers and other three-dimensional elements. Basic instructions are included for piecing the quilt top.

I haven't included yardage amounts for the fabrics. No one piece needs much, except for the background. I encourage you to use a lot of different fabrics, even if they don't match perfectly.

Inspiration for Garden at Dusk was a pieced quilt of bright flowers on a mid- to dark blue background pictured in a magazine. I thought how much easier the quilt would be to make using three-dimensional piecing. After completing the quilt, I happened upon the original picture in the magazine, and I was amazed at how much my quilt differed from the picture.

The finished size of the Garden at Dusk quilt is 38″ (96.5 cm) × 28″ (71 cm).

Materials

Green fabrics for the garden background
Blue fabrics for the sky background
Scraps of fabrics for the sun, tree, leaves, flowers, bird, potting shed, potting shed door and latch, and watering can
Matching thread
Bead for bird's eye
Scraps of yarn for hollyhocks
1 yard (.92 m) fabric for backing
⅜ yard (.35 m) fabric for binding
Batting

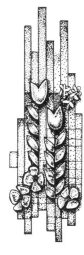

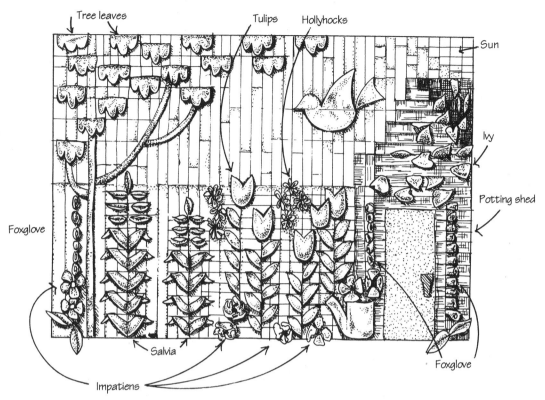

Fig. 12-1 *Garden at Dusk*

Go For It!

Creativity doesn't require any special knowledge. For instance, I don't know any rules about color and have not taken any quilting classes. Rather, I've learned to have confidence in my intuition. I believe I owe my success to the fact that I don't think I *can't* do it, and therefore I try. (Thanks, Mom.)

Creativity is a way of thinking and seeing. Design is putting that vision into one form or another. If you think that's magic, you're right. But like any trick, the magician has a logical explanation. Most magicians guard their secrets carefully, but I've shared mine. Now, create some magic of your own!

Instructions

Note: All seam allowances are ¼" (6 mm) unless specified otherwise. Patterns appear at the end of the chapter.

1. Prepare the fabrics and patterns as instructed in "Fabric Preparation" and "How to Transfer Patterns" in The Basics.

2. Cut the sky and garden background fabrics into 1½"- (4 cm) wide strips.

3. Cut one 18½" (46.8 cm) × 1½" (4 cm) strip from the tree trunk fabric. For the tree branches, cut 2"- (5 cm) wide bias strips from the same fabric. Cut some 1½"- (4 cm) wide brown strips for the potting shed and roof. For the sun, cut 20 yellow 1½" (4 cm) squares from various fabrics.

4. To make the tree leaves; both ivy leaves; foxglove leaves; impatiens flower petals; salvia leaf tips; and the bird's head, tail, body, and wing, do the following: With right sides facing, stitch the two fabric pieces as indicated on the pattern, leaving the marked edge open (Fig. 12-2). Trim seam allowances to ⅛" (3 mm). Turn each sewn piece right side out.

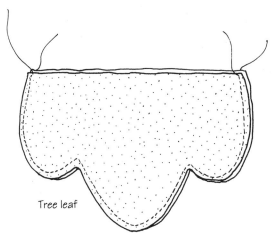

Tree leaf

Fig. 12-2 *With right sides facing, stitch, leaving the designated edge unstitched for turning. Turn the sewn piece right side out. The open edge will be inserted into a background seam.*

5. To make the tulip, tulip leaf, door latch, and salvia leaf, do the following: With right sides facing, stitch the two fabric pieces together along opposite edges, leaving the two ends open as indicated on the pattern (Fig. 12-3). Trim seam allowances to ⅛" (3 mm). Turn each sewn piece right side out.

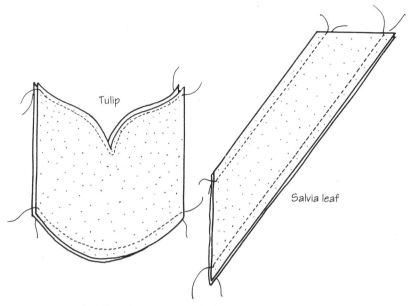

Fig. 12-3 *With right sides facing, stitch the two pieces together along two opposite edges, leaving the other two ends open. Turn the sewn piece right side out. The unstitched ends will be inserted into the background.*

6. To make the salvia flower, stitch two salvia fabric pieces together, right sides facing. Trim the seam allowances to ⅛″ (3 mm). Make a slash in the back layer of fabric at the center as indicated on the pattern. Trim seam allowances to ⅛″ (3 mm). Turn the flower right side out (Fig. 12-4).

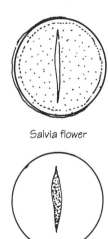

Fig. 12-4 *For each salvia flower, stitch two salvia fabric pieces together, right sides facing. Make a slash at the center of one layer of fabric and turn the flower right side out.*

7. Starting at the left-hand side of the quilt, start piecing the various sections of the quilt: the background, the tree trunk, the potting shed, and the sun. Piece the background strips into sections wherever a leaf or flower dictates (Fig. 12-5). Following the quilt diagram in Figure 12-1, the color photo of the quilt, or your own intuition, insert a leaf, flower, or other element in the seams at the appropriate places. Figures 12-6 through 12-16 give specific directions for inserting most of the elements.

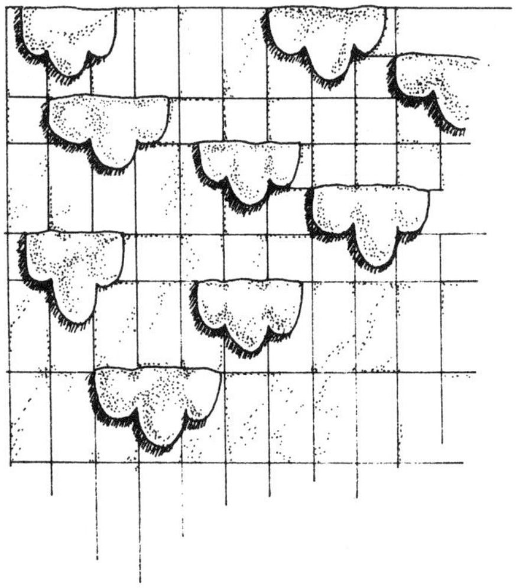

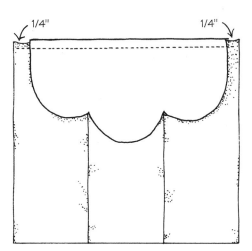

Fig. 12-5 *Piece the background in sections following the quilt diagram in Figure 12-1. Allow the leaves and flowers to dictate the way you piece the background. Insert leaves, flowers, and other design elements into seams as you construct the quilt top.*

Fig. 12-6 *Stitch the tree leaf into a seam across three vertical background strips.*

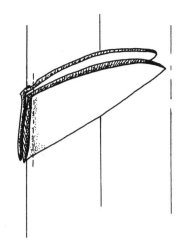

Fig. 12-7 *Fold two foxglove leaves in half lengthwise. Pair them and insert both into a vertical seam.*

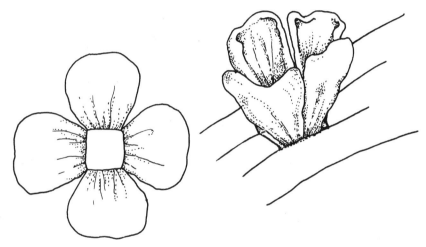

Fig. 12-8 *Cut a 1½" (4 cm) square flower center for each impatiens. Gather an impatiens petal to each side of the center square. (It's a very tight fit.) Stitch the center square into a background seam.*

Foxglove flower top

Wrong side of fabric

Fig. 12-9 *To make a foxglove flower, cut a 3½" (9 cm) square. (I made flowers from two fabrics.) With right sides facing, stitch two edges of the flower together. Start turning the flower right side out but stop halfway so that the fold creates the top of the flower. Pin the raw edges together and insert them into a background seam at an angle.*

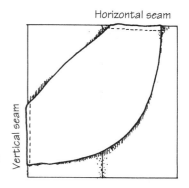

Fig. 12-10 *Stitch the lower end of the tulip leaves into a vertical background seam and the upper edge into a horizontal background seam.*

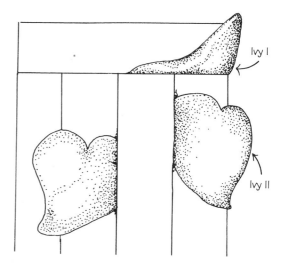

Fig. 12-11 *Stitch the ivy leaves into vertical and horizontal background seams.*

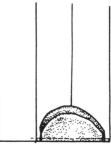

Fig. 12-12 *Fold each salvia flower along its slash, keeping the slash on the outside. Insert the folded edge into a seam in the background.*

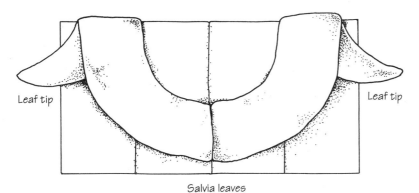

Salvia leaves

Fig. 12-13 *Stitch the lower open edges of two salvia leaves into a vertical seam. Before stitching the upper open edges of the leaves into horizontal seams, slip a salvia leaf tip under the upper end of each leaf.*

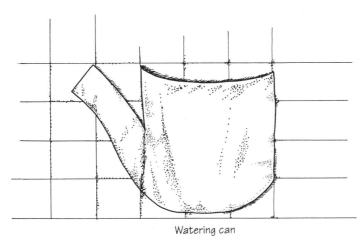

Watering can

Fig. 12-14 *Cut two 4½" (11.5 cm) squares for the watering can. With right sides facing, stitch the top and bottom edges. Turn the square right side out. Use the salvia leaf pattern to make the spout. Leave only one short edge of the spout unstitched. Insert the unfinished two edges of the watering can into vertical seams, 3" (7.5 cm) apart. Insert the unstitched edge of the spout into the bottom of one of these vertical seams and leave the top edge of the spout free. Stitch the seams.*

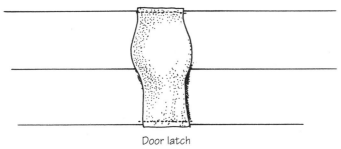

Door latch

Fig. 12-15 *Stitch the unstitched ends of the door latch into horizontal seams in the potting shed door. Leave some slack so that the handle bows out slightly.*

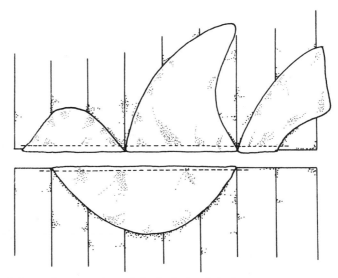

Fig. 12-16 *Insert the open edges of the bird's head, body, wings, and tail into adjoining horizontal seams. Restitch the seams. Press the pieces into their proper positions. Tack the wing and tail tips to the quilt top. Stitch the bead for the bird's eye in place.*

8. Piece the sections together to form a complete quilt top. Some elements can be added after the entire quilt top is stitched together—for example, the tree branches. To make the tree branches, stitch the long edges of the 2″- (5 cm) wide bias strips together. Turn the strips right side out. Press. Open the background seams at the tree trunk and tree leaf where you wish to insert the tree branches and restitch the seams with the ends of the branches inserted (Fig. 12-17).

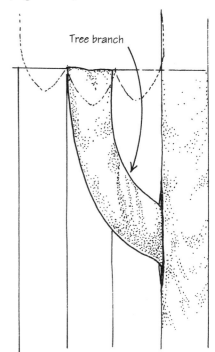

Tree branch

Fig. 12-17 *Decide where you want to add a tree branch. Tear open the seams at the leaf and trunk. Insert the ends of the branch. Restitch the seams. Trim the extra ends of the branch.*

9. Hollyhocks also can be added after the quilt top is constructed. To make the hollyhocks, wind two pieces of yarn loosely around two fingers about eight times. Remove the yarn from your fingers. Tie a piece of yarn around the center of the wound yarn (Fig. 12-18). Tack the hollyhocks onto the completed quilt top.

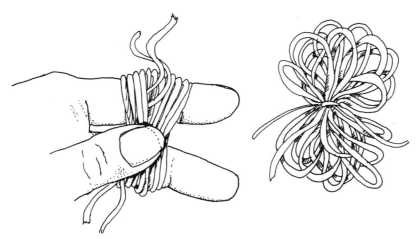

Fig. 12-18 *Create the hollyhocks by wrapping yarn around your fingers, tying the bundle of yarn, and tacking the bundle to the quilt top.*

10. Layer the quilt top, batting, and backing. Quilt. The large number of three-dimensional pieces in this quilt dictate a minimal amount of quilting. For the sky, I quilted horizontal waves that dodge the leaves and the bird. For the garden, I stitched in the ditch vertically along the stems. I also stitched around the door and sides of the potting shed. Bind.

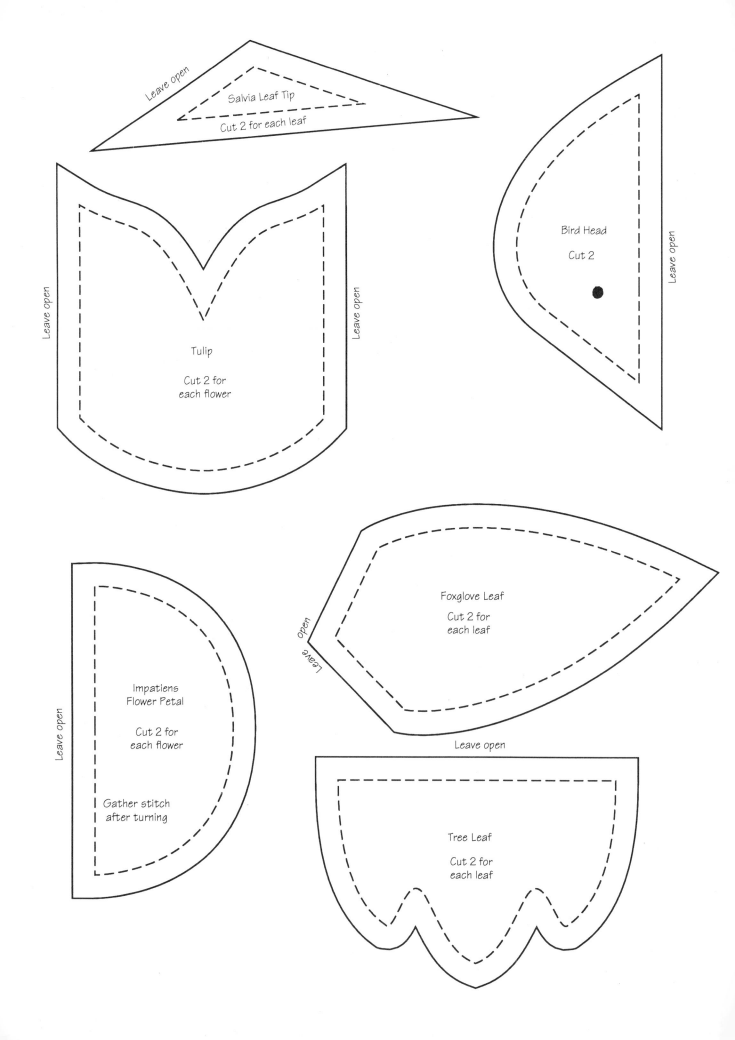

Leave open

Salvia Leaf Tip

Cut 2 for each leaf

Leave open

Bird Head

Cut 2

Leave open

Leave open

Leave open

Tulip

Cut 2 for
each flower

Foxglove Leaf

Cut 2 for
each leaf

Leave open

Leave open

Impatiens
Flower Petal

Cut 2 for
each flower

Gather stitch
after turning

Leave open

Tree Leaf

Cut 2 for
each leaf

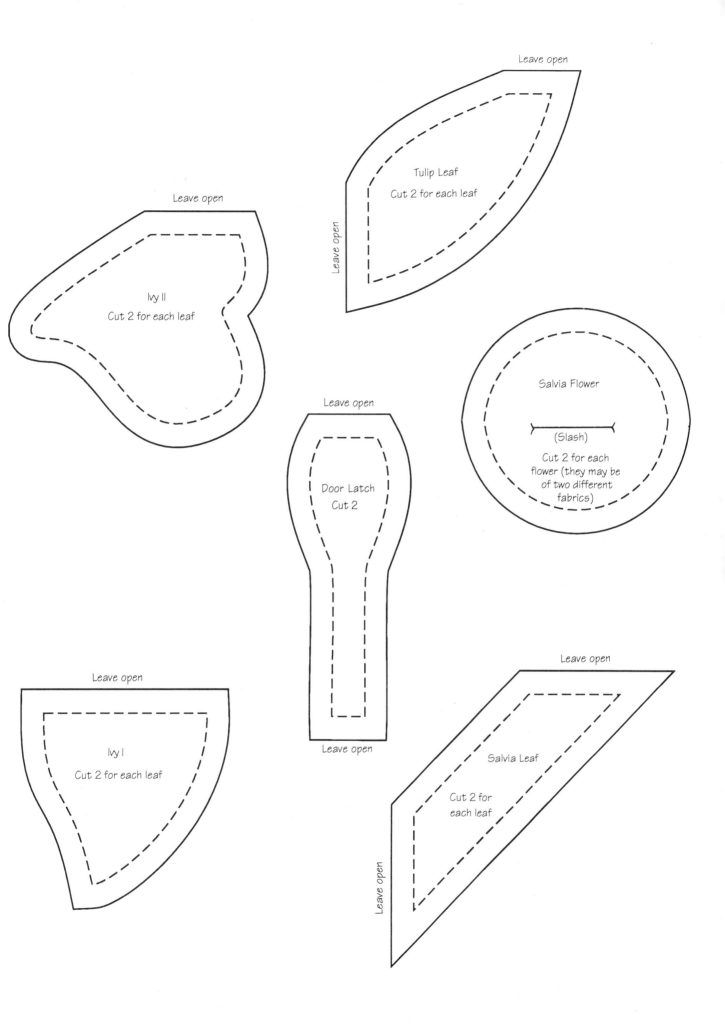

Leave open

Tulip Leaf
Cut 2 for each leaf

Leave open

Leave open

Ivy II
Cut 2 for each leaf

Salvia Flower

(Slash)

Cut 2 for each
flower (they may be
of two different
fabrics)

Leave open

Door Latch
Cut 2

Leave open

Leave open

Ivy I
Cut 2 for each leaf

Leave open

Salvia Leaf

Cut 2 for
each leaf

Leave open

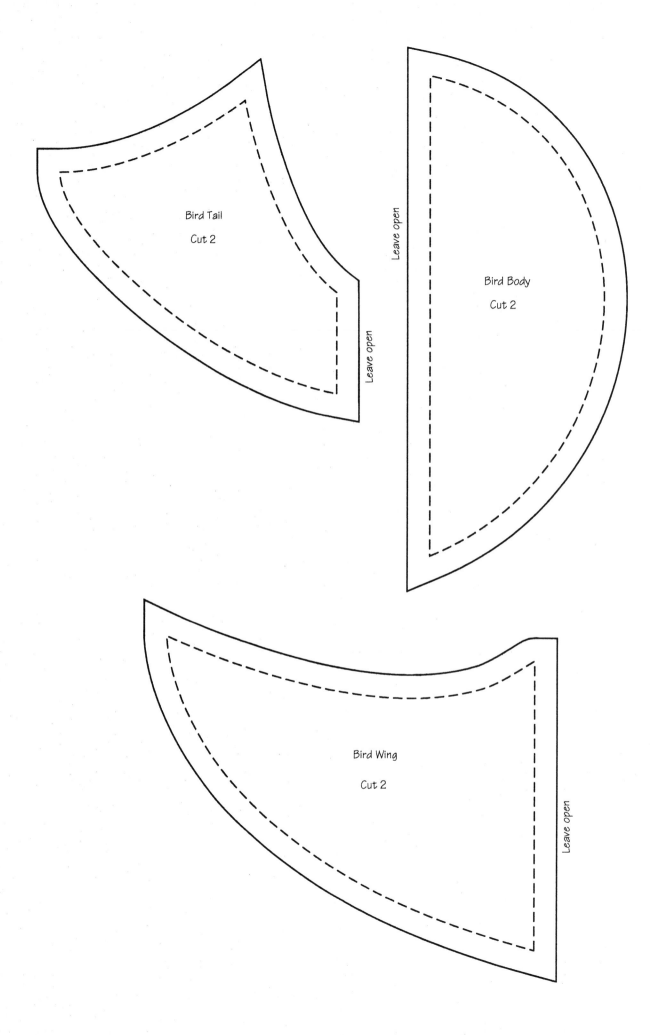

An Invitation

You'd think that after designing the quilts for both *Three-Dimensional Appliqué* and *Three-Dimensional Pieced Quilts*, the Quilt Muse would be sated and the 3-D ideas would slow down their wild orbits in my head. Not so. Now the Muse is hankering to combine piecing and appliqué in quilts. Oh, so many more ideas!

My hope in writing these books is that your creativity will be similarly peaked. Whether you follow the instructions within these pages to the word, or use the ideas to travel along your own path, I'd love to see the results. If I share your creations with others, I'll be sure to give you full credit.

Please send letters, photos, comments, criticism to me at:

Jodie Davis
P.O. Box 673
Gainesville, VA 22065

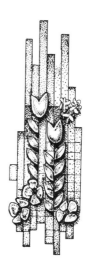

Sources

American Beauty Fabrics
610 Hamilton Pkwy.
DeWitt, NY 13214

Source for hand-dyed fabrics used in swirling fans.

Cabin Fever Calicoes
P.O. Box 550106
Atlanta, GA 30355
(800) 762-2246
Catalog: $2.50

Fabrics, quilting supplies.

Clotilde Inc.
2 Sew Smart Way
Stevens Point, WI 54481
(800) 772-2891
Catalog: Free

Sewing supplies at a 20% discount. Source for the Stuff-It tool.

Dover St. Booksellers
39 East Dover Street
Box 1563
Easton, MD 21601
Catalog: $2.00

Quilting books.

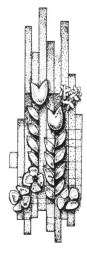

G Street Fabrics Mail Order
   Service
12240 Wilkins Avenue
Rockville, MD 20852
(301) 231-8960

Color cards with samplings of some of the hundreds of quilting fabric they carry. Visit if you ever get a chance.

Home Sew
P.O. Box 4099
Bethlehem, PA 18018
Catalog: Free

I used the 4" Battenberg doilies from Home Sew in the Flower Basket quilt. Wonderful prices.

Keepsake Quilting
Dover Street
P.O. Box 1459
Meredith, NH 03253
Catalog: Free, or $1 for first-class
   mail

Quilting supplies and fabrics. Carries the Stuff-It tool.

Nancy's Notions, Ltd.
P.O. Box 683
Beaver Dam, WI 53916-0683
(800) 833-0690
Catalog: Free

Sewing supplies and videos.

Purchase For Less
231 Floresta PFL
Portola Valley, CA 94028
Catalog: $2.00

Save 20%–40% on selected quilting and sewing books.

Quilts & Other Comforts
P.O. Box 394-223
Wheatridge, CO 80034-0394
Catalog: $2.50

Quilting supplies.

Quilting Books Unlimited
1911 West Wilson
Batavia, IL 60510
(708) 406-0237
Booklist: $1.00

Stitch 'N Craft Supply
5634 West Meadowbrook
Phoenix, AZ 85031
(800) 279-1995

For $25 a year, membership in this club allows you (and a friend—you may combine your orders under one name and membership fee) to enjoy incredible savings on sewing and quilting supplies, books, thread, batting, and more.

Bibliography

Beyer, Jinny. *The Quilter's Album of Blocks and Borders*. McLean, Va.: EPM Publications, Inc., 1986.

Fanning, Robbie, and Tony Fanning. *The Complete Book of Machine Quilting, 2nd edition*. Radnor, Pa.: Chilton Book Company, 1994.

Fons, Marianne, and Liz Porter. *Quilter's Complete Guide*. Birmingham, Ala.: Oxmoor House, 1993.

Hargrave, Harriet. *Heirloom Machine Quilting*. Lafayette, Calif.: C&T Publishing, 1990.

Singer Sewing Reference Library. *Quilting By Machine*. Minnetonka, Minn.: Cy DeCosse Inc., 1990.

Saunders, Jan. *Teach Yourself to Sew Better: A Step-by-Step Guide to Your Sewing Machine*. Radnor, Pa.: Chilton Book Company, 1990.

Smith, Lois. *Fun and Fancy Machine Quiltmaking*. Paducah, Ky.: American Quilter's Society, 1989.

Soltow, Willow Ann. *Designing Your Own Quilts*. Radnor, Pa.: Chilton Book Company, 1993.

Thomas, Donna Lynn. *A Perfect Match: A Guide to Precise Machine Piecing*. Bothell, Wash.: That Patchwork Place, 1993.

Wagner, Debra. *Teach Yourself Machine Piecing and Quilting*. Radnor, Pa.: Chilton Book Company, 1992.

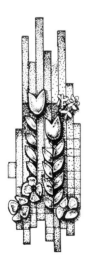